LEAP OF FAITH

QUIT YOUR JOB AND LIVE ON A BOAT

D0631961

ED ROBINSON

outskirtspress

DENVER, COLORADO

Leap of Faith
Quit Your Job and Live on a Boat
All Rights Reserved.
Copyright © 2013 Ed Robinson
v3.0

Outskirts Press, Inc.
http://www.outskirtspress.com

ISBN: 978-1-4787-2092-8

Outskirts Press and the "OP" logo are trademarks belonging to Outskirts Press, Inc.

PRINTED IN THE UNITED STATES OF AMERICA

For the lovely Miss Kim.

TABLE OF CONTENTS

PRELUDE

I live the greatest life that's ever been lived.

There is a song by the Zac Brown Band where Jimmy Buffett himself sings, "Wrote a note said be back in a minute. Bought a boat and I sailed off in it." Well, I did just that. Now I am the happiest person on the face of the earth.

If there is anyone who can truly claim to live the life that Jimmy sings about, it is me. You can too. I have a story to tell, from nuts and bolts to anecdotes. The how-tos and the why-fors of achieving a dream life are in these pages.

Come on along. Enjoy the ride.

1

THE GOOD LIFE

What's so great about living on a boat? What's so special about my life in particular you ask? Let's consider a typical day in the life of the happiest guy in the world.

As I write, I'm sitting on the back of my yacht. The boat is anchored in a slice of Eden known as Pelican Bay. She's nestled snugly between the beautiful island of Cayo Costa and the patch of sand and mangroves named Punta Blanca Island. The sun is shining in an impossibly crystal blue sky. It's eighty-four degrees, the water is flat and clear, and I just cracked open an ice cold beer.

I've got my feet propped up on the transom. It's time to reflect on my day. It's Happy Hour, after five but before sunset.

Before dawn this morning, I took my coffee in this same spot, same pose as a matter of fact. There was just enough light to make out the dolphins nearby hunting for breakfast. Those I didn't see I could still hear each time they surfaced for air. It was still, peaceful and quiet. The lack of noise is profound. No cars, no trucks, no sirens, no backing trash trucks going beep, beep, beep. None of the sounds that dirt dwellers become accustomed to are heard here. They are replaced by the breath of dolphins. I can here ospreys chirping from the island. Occasionally there's a splash from a pelican diving on bait.

That reminds me of another song by my favorite singer/songwriter Jim Morris. "Pelicans diving crashing on bait, pretty soon the dolphins arrive. I move down the shoreline and hear a snook pop, oh the mangroves are coming alive." Those are the sounds I hear.

Eventually the sun peaks its head over the eastern horizon. I snap a picture to share with my Facebook following. Lots of them tell me they would never see a sunrise if not for my pictures. Most mornings after I catch a spectacular sunrise, I'll head off in the dinghy in search of redfish, snook, tarpon, trout, grouper, cobia, snapper or whatever I can find. Fishing gives me great joy. Legal fish that are good to eat may become tonight's dinner, but it also keeps me in close proximity to nature's beauty that is all around me. I may see more dolphin, or manatees, or rolling tarpon. I may sit and float and just take it all in, letting the breeze take me wherever it wants to go.

On these quiet mornings, I could be lost in concentration trying to sneak up on a wily fish in shallow water. The world is blocked out. It's just me, my spinning rod and the fish. Or I could be totally aware of my surroundings, my eyes awake to every aspect of flora and fauna in this special place.

Afternoons I spend with my beautiful wife. She's a tall, thin blonde who at age forty-seven still looks great in a bikini. After a late breakfast or early lunch we head off to the beach together. It's not just any beach. It's white sand and clear blue water. More importantly, it's empty of other people. It seems impossible that such a heavenly place isn't overrun with tourists, especially in Florida, but here it is. We have our very own private beach. Okay so there are a few tourists about three miles away. They get dropped off by ferry boats near the north end, but we never see them here. On weekends, we occasionally encounter locals in their own boats who anchor near shore. On even more rare occasions we'll meet folks like us. I guess there are few cruisers who know about this secluded beach, but very few. Most of the time there is no one here but the two of us.

Our beach routine varies, but it always begins with a moment of standing and staring. It's so beautiful here, like a postcard. This beach is as nice as any in the Caribbean, and it's all ours. We look north at white sand with no sign of another human. We look south and can just make out North Captiva Island. We see the calm blue Gulf of Mexico stretching out to the horizon.

We set up our beach chairs, admire each other's ridiculously deep tan and just smile. Some days we walk. Some days we hunt for sea shells. I've developed a knack for finding sand dollars. The lovely Miss Kim is always the first to find starfish. Some days we just sit and read. Some days I'll fish a little off the beach. Whenever I'm out here with a fishing rod, I can hear Jim Morris singing in my head. "The Cayo Costa is quiet this morning. It's so good to be back on my turf. I walk through the sand, fly rod in hand, just looking for snook in the surf."

Every day we are back on the boat by five o'clock, because that's Happy Hour. We shower up if it's necessary. I grab a cold beer, Kim fills a tumbler with box-o-wine, then we clink can to plastic and make a toast to another day in paradise. Later on we'll have some nips of rum.

Then it's time for the sunset. We celebrate it, each and every night. It's an important ritual all across Florida that you'll read more about later. Somewhere in there we eat dinner, but it's usually an afterthought, just sustenance. Some nights after dark we get naked and have mad monkey sex. Other nights we get naked and make sweet gentle love. Every night we sleep the sleep of the contented.

That's what it's like to be me. Can you see how I feel justified in claiming to live the greatest life that's ever been lived?

2

SMILING OUT LOUD

Some folks say I like to live my life like a Jimmy Buffett song. I actually prefer to say I like to live my life like a Jim Morris song. Here's a little bit of one:

He moved down from Long Island

He's living out in Pelican Bay

He's got a spot right on the water

He's got no rent to pay.

He's got no fussy neighbors

No gate no security guards

He fishes from his front porch

SMILING OUT LOUD

He's got the beach in his back yard.

It always seemed like a good idea

Buy a little houseboat free and clear

Living on Shrimp and Navagator Beer

Every day goes by without a cloud

And every time you see him

He's smiling out loud.

Yep, that's me. I listened to the songs and now I live them. But how did I get here? It all started with Travis McGee over twenty years ago. Prolific author John D. MacDonald wrote twenty-one books starring the tough guy hero. Travis always killed the bad guys and slept with the pretty women. I read all of them and he was my personal hero for several reasons.

In addition to his action filled exploits, Travis lived on a fifty-two foot barge type houseboat called the Busted Flush. He won it in a poker game and tied it up in slip F-18, Bahia Mar Marina in Fort Lauderdale. He went fishing often and admired the fish he caught, occasionally keeping one for dinner but more often releasing them. He mourned the loss of Old Florida, hating the development and draining of the swamps. He also despised the greed and corruption of said developers and politicians. He stood up for what was right. He helped those in need.

All that sounded pretty awesome to me, but there was one thing that intrigued me about Travis. He was taking his retirement in installments. He only took a case when the money ran low, or if he got guilted into helping someone (usually a sexy babe). In between jobs he lived a sweet life. He was a beach bum, a fisherman, a drinker but not a drunk. I wanted to be just like him.

It took many long years for me to figure out how, but as of today I haven't worked in over two and a half years. I've been living a life of leisure in a warm and sunny place. I'm a beach bum, a fisherman, a drinker but not a drunk. I've still got a little money in the bank. I'm only fifty years old.

Could you go thirty months or more without a paycheck and survive with cash to spare? I know that you think you can't, that it's impossible. You are wrong. You can do it. Maybe not right now, but eventually you can.

We'll get to that soon enough.

3

WHO IS JIM MORRIS?

At this point I figure there are some readers thinking, who the hell is Jim Morris? Why is he important to this story? Well, Jim and his music are essential to telling my tale.

Six or seven years ago, a friend handed me two CDs. He said he thought I might like the guy. I loved the songs. I bought a few more and they became all I listened to. It's a slice of the island life. It's quitting your job and running away music. It's clear blue water and a quart of rum. It's fishing and sailing and white sand beaches with a big ole jug of sangria wine.

Some guy I'd never heard of was changing my life with his music so I checked him out further. He tours the country some but is very popular in Florida. In one song he tags himself as a semi-significant star. I discovered that he and his band played nearby occasionally on the East Coast swing. One cold January day we made our way to the Jetty Dock Bar on Maryland's eastern shore for our first taste of Jim Morris and The Big Bamboo Band. I was surprised by the huge crowd and their enthusiasm. It was like nothing I'd ever seen before. My wife and I were both hooked. It was more fun than a Jimmy Buffett concert, if that's possible.

We saw them play a few more times and eventually graduated from Parrotheads to Bocanuts, as his fans are called. Kim and I were engaged at the time, and I came up with a brilliant plan for our wedding. I contacted Jim and asked if we could marry on his stage when he returned to the Jetty. He agreed and I made the arrangements. When the day came we had not only our friends and family present, but also a few hundred strangers.

The crowd started growing

The place started swinging

The beer started flowing

Everybody started singing

(From Navagator Afternoon, by Jim Morris)

It was like having the reception before the wedding, then a huge party afterwards. Jim was so gracious to allow it. The staff at The Jetty was very accommodating. Miss Kim was so beautiful. I couldn't dream of a better way to begin our new life together. I had no idea at the time, but it would only get better. I also didn't know how much more of a role Jim would play in shaping our future.

For our first vacation as a married couple we chose Punta Gorda, Florida. Jim holds his own music festival there annually. We arrived early so we could do the tourist thing before it began. We hit Sanibel, Boca Grande, and Fisherman's Village. We even rented a boat and drove it out to Pelican Bay where we now live.

I saw where Jim was playing at Bert's Bar in Matlacha. It billed itself as the ultimate dive bar with a million dollar view. That's my kind of place. Jim recognized us and we spoke. As we exchanged pleasantries he said, "Wait a minute, I'll be right back." He returned with another couple who also lived in Maryland. Introductions were made and we spent the rest of the show drinking and sharing stories. They became fast friends, thanks to Jim. Later, when we made our move to Punta Gorda, we stayed in their condo while boat shopping. They acted as our tour guides and mentors while we were still new in town. They remain great friends to this day.

I can't count how many other fine people we've met along the way thanks to Jim and his music. There are so many that we now call friends who we met at one of his shows. They further enrich our wonderful lives.

4

SEEKING SOMETHING MORE

It wasn't always this way. I lived like everyone else. I had a good job, but I had grown to hate it. I had bills, lots of them. There was rent to pay, truck payment, credit card bills and the accumulation of stuff. It was cold in the winter and it snowed a lot. I had good friends, a few of them great. I had a good, normal life. I was trudging along like everyone does.

I did everything life asked of me. I worked hard, won some measure of success. I bought whatever toys I thought I wanted. It never seemed like it was enough. Is that all there is to life? I had a pretty wife who loved me. I had a great daughter I was proud of. She was all grown up and a great parent herself. The job was secure. I probably could have stayed on until proper retirement or death, except that it was driving me insane.

I couldn't shake the feeling that there ought to be something more. I found myself daydreaming more and more. I fantasized about chucking it all and running away. I explored job opportunities in Florida. I researched boats on the internet.

Not that I wasn't happy. I felt fortunate. I had it better than most and I knew it. There was just some inner yearning for freedom. As good as my life was, it wasn't exactly what I had planned. I just sort of ended up there. Through choices both good and bad, circumstances unforeseen, and good luck and bad luck, one day you wake up and realize this is where you ended up. That's how it works for most everyone.

It became clear to me that most folks, if they even realize the same thing, simply choose to accept their fate. Keep on keeping on. Keep showing up for work. Pay the bills. Save a little something for retirement if you live that long. Put one foot in front of the other. Get out of bed. Go to work. Watch television. Go to bed. Rinse and repeat.

It's just the way the world works. What else is there? I pondered that question for a long time. The daydreaming continued. The island songs played on. The job felt more and more like an anchor all the time. Did I mention it snowed a lot?

I wish I could tell you about one single moment when I had a great epiphany, that instant in time when I said, "Screw it. I'm quitting my job and going off to live on a boat." It didn't work that way. Society itself was holding me back. The normal, responsible thing to do was keep trudging right along. Hold on to all you've worked for. Accept your fate. Settle in to your middle class American existence. Hope you don't get cancer before you can retire for a few years in your old age.

Yes I pondered all that endlessly, especially the cancer possibility. My mother lost a brief and brutal battle with breast cancer at the age of fifty-seven. My sister got to live to the ripe old age of fifty before kidney and liver cancer took her. Dad actually did get to retire. He got almost ten years of living his dream before pancreatic cancer took him at seventy-two. So I figured I had twenty more years optimistically. Possibly I had a whole lot less.

How was I going to live it? I need to find a way to chart my own course. I couldn't let life decide for me how thing were going to turn out. I wanted to control my own destiny. I wasn't quite sure how, but I was going to figure it out. I was going to live life as I chose.

5

LIVING FOR TODAY

How am I living today? Today was pretty sweet. After my morning coffee with dolphins, which I never tire of, I finished up an excellent novel. There are many great Florida authors that write about many of the places I go. It enhances my reading experience when my feet are propped up on my boat, especially when the characters visit an island I can see from where I'm anchored. I then did a little writing of my own.

By early afternoon there remained only one other boat here in Pelican Bay. We've become very good friends with the couple who live aboard it. The guy went through his own bout with cancer in the form of brain tumors. He kicked cancers ass. Now here is a person who truly lives for today. He is one of those rare people who enjoy life to the fullest.

LIVING FOR TODAY

The four of us took our dinghies three miles south to the island of Cabbage Key. Every tourist who comes near this part of the world ends up at Cabbage Key eventually, which is why we rarely visit. It was off-season, mid-afternoon on a Monday. We found the place empty. That's how we like it.

The Inn at Cabbage Key sits atop an ancient Indian shell mound. You can only get there by boat. The walls of the bar are plastered with dollar bills by the tens of thousands. Visitors are encouraged to sign a dollar with magic marker and tape it to the wall. Nary a square inch of wall space isn't covered layers deep.

The staff is friendly and the view is magnificent. We had the bar to ourselves so the bartender had time to share a few stories. They claim this is where Jimmy Buffett wrote Cheeseburger in Paradise. His autographed picture hangs on the wall behind the bar.

After a few beers we head back. A dinghy race is on! Their fifteen horsepower Yamaha proved too much for our 9.9 Mercury. We made quick pit stops at our boats to load coolers with beer, wine and rum. Then we regrouped on the sand spit at the northern entrance to Pelican Bay. It's a low, narrow strip of sand and shell that's perfect for landing a dinghy or small boat.

We sat in the clean water drinking beer and swapping stories until the sun went down. For those few hours there was no one else on Earth. There were no mass shootings, no politics, no gossip or bills to pay. There were only four good friends getting slightly high on the sun, water, sand and companionship. The booze probably had a little to do with it as well.

We were in a world of our own, far separated from society. We laughed and drank and we lingered in the glow. Pelicans perched on the tip of the peninsula. Fish swam right by our toes in the clear water. A white heron grew comfortable with our presence and drew close enough to touch. It was many moments of magic in a southwest Florida paradise. It only came to an end due to approaching darkness and a dwindling beer supply. Yes today was mighty fine. That is how I've chosen to live my life.

6

SEEDS OF A PLAN

*"I'd rather be here just drinking a beer
than freezing my ass in the North,"*

(Michael McCloud, The Conch
Republic National Anthem)

Every day spent living a dream in Paradise is better than
those days I spent at work in the North. By anyone's
standards it was a great job with excellent pay, good
benefits, company vehicle and matching 401K. No one
in their right mind would simply walk away from such
a good position. I had worked hard for many years to
get where I was. I was being handsomely rewarded.

On the other hand, there were crazy employees, bellig-
erent customers, broken down equipment and corporate

politics. There was one problem after another. It was my job to solve them. I'd put out one fire and two more would ignite. Challenges came from all directions, at any time of day or night. Every day of the year came the responsibility to make the decisions. I held hands and kicked asses. I kept putting out the fires.

When I was younger and more ambitious career-wise, I ate that kind of stress for lunch. Give me a full-sized order of problems to go please, with a shot of tequila. As I got a little older and began fantasizing about a mystical live-aboard life in the islands, the stress started eating me. Can I get a diet portion of problems please, with a side of Prilosec?

I'd come home in the evenings and spend twenty minutes bitching and moaning to my ever patient wife. God bless her. Then I'd lie down on the couch. Not because I was sleepy, I was mentally exhausted. I could escape for an hour, if my phone didn't ring. Then I'd sit and drink beer in front of the television until bedtime. Get up and do it all again tomorrow. I had to find a way out. It was sucking at my soul.

I always considered myself a little contrary to ordinary. I tended to follow a slightly different path than most others did. But this, this was going to take balls, big brass ones. It was going to take time, planning and money. It was going to require one giant leap of faith.

SEEDS OF A PLAN

Can I pull it off? What's it really like living on a boat? It sounds fun and romantic, but what if it's hard, uncomfortable or even dangerous? Can I really just quit my job? I'll be giving up my income and my security. Are my balls big enough? What do I do for money? What if it all goes wrong?

You've got to start somewhere, so I set out to find the answers to as many of those questions as I could. I began my quest with research. I really had no idea what it was going to take. I had lived my life around water and boats, but living on one? I owned boats. I loved spending time on them, but had never ventured from the familiar waters of the Chesapeake and Delaware Bays. I was going to have to educate myself.

I found books on the subject, written by those intrepid souls who had already made the leap. I read magazines and visited websites. I absorbed every bit of information I could find about living aboard and cruising. I read technical stuff about boat systems. I read about diesel engines, generators, water makers, solar panels, wind generators and proper anchoring technique. I read fun stuff about having too many mangos, palm trees and the ocean breeze, clear blue waters and cloud-proof skies.

All that reading started to improve my mood. I felt that I was doing something to move towards achieving my ultimate goal. Sure it was a small step, but it really helped make the dream seem possible. Others had done it, were doing it. I could do it too.

My education on living the life was progressing nicely, but solutions to the money issue were few. Mostly, cruisers were retired with some income. I was nowhere near retirement age. I didn't want to wait that long. I wanted to take my retirement while I was young enough to enjoy it fully. I wanted to be like Travis McGee but I had no money.

Like so many Americans today, every dollar I made, I spent. I looked around and took stock of all of the things I had spent my hard earned money on. I had everything I ever wanted. Kim never knew what to buy me for Christmas because if I ever wanted something, I had already bought it. As far as material possessions went, I lacked nothing, yet it was never enough.

It was time to change my priorities. If I wanted to achieve my dreams I was going to have to rethink how I handled money. I needed to reconsider the value of my possessions.

It was time to get serious. Money needs to work for me, instead of me working for money.

7

DEBT FREE EQUALS FREEDOM

We live in a consumer driven society. Consumer spending is approximately seventy percent of all economic growth. What does that mean exactly? It means that the health of our economy depends on all of us to continue to buy stuff. Most of us buy stuff like our own lives depended on it.

We trade in our perfectly satisfactory, slight used car for the hottest new model every few years. Our old thirty-six inch television is just nothing compared to our new fifty inch LCD model. We stand in line for the newest Iphone to replace our ancient one year old Blackberry. We buy Ipods for music and Ipads for internet on the go. We buy boats or campers or both. We have a four-wheeler in the garage that we rarely ride. We buy a

Harley Davidson then almost immediately start lusting after a bigger, better Harley. We buy Longaberger baskets and jewelry. We want new clothes, new shoes, new artwork for the walls.

We refinance our homes in order to put in a swimming pool or build an addition. We need the addition to house all the stuff we bought. We can't park our car in the garage because it's too full of stuff. We buy a shed to put our John Deere mower in. We even rent storage space to store all the overflow of stuff. We use our credit cards to take a vacation, leave our shiny new stuff behind for a week.

In my case, I owned dozens of the finest fishing rods money can buy, but if I could just add that three hundred dollar G Loomis rod to my collection, then I'd be happy.

It's getting worse all the time, and it's fueled by debt. In 1975, household debt as a percentage of Gross Domestic Product was forty-five percent. By 2009, that figured had increased to ninety-six percent. In 1975, household debt as a percentage of disposable income was sixty-two percent. We still owned more than we owed. By 2009, that figure exploded to one-hundred and twenty-three percent. We now owe more than we own, much more.

DEBT FREE EQUALS FREEDOM

We've all been indoctrinated into the culture of spending since birth. Every aspect of modern American society encourages us to buy more and more stuff. Everyone watches hours of television daily and subjects themselves to an endless barrage of advertising. Magazines, billboards, movies, radio, newspapers and even the internet implore you to purchase products. "Keeping up with the Jones" has become a national obsession. Our sense of worth is tied to the things we can buy.

It's a great big lie and we all bought in to it, literally.

Are we any happier now that we've accumulated all this crap? For the most part, the answer to that is no. Do you really need another Longaberger basket? Do you really need a new smartphone or another new fishing rod? No, no and no, you don't.

So here is step number one on the path to financial freedom from the happiest man on Earth . . . stop buying stuff. Stop buying stuff unless it's food, basic necessities or maybe a book on how to live your dream.

That's the easy part. Step number two is much tougher, but absolutely essential. Pay off your debt. Pay it all off, right now, as fast as possible. This will require radical changes to how you handle money. It will affect how you live. It will require self discipline and perseverance. You must completely change your mindset and stay determined.

You will need to reassess all of the things you own. Do you owe money on that four-wheeler in the garage? Sell it. Pay off the loan. Do you own it outright? Great, sell it. Use the money to pay off credit card debt. What other toys or luxuries do you have? Boats, campers, motorcycles, they all have to go. You won't need them where you are going. You'll be walking off one day with nothing but some clothes. You will be free.

Every time you rid yourself of an asset, you'll have more money. Either you will have saved yourself the amount of the loan payment or taken a cash windfall if you owned it free and clear. Take that money and apply it to some other debt. Use the amount of the loan payment to pay extra on your car payment each month. Use any extra cash the same way. Put it straight to the principle on your car loan or pay down credit cards. Any and all money from the sale of your toys must go only to pay down debt.

This is going to be a challenge. You are giving up your precious belongings. You're not spending that money on shiny new things. You will need to separate your self-worth from the objects you bought. **Debt free equals freedom**. That is your ultimate goal.

Becoming debt free took me almost four years. I wasn't in that bad of shape. It may take you longer, but you've got to start today. It may be as simple as not buying a new car. When you pay yours off, take that extra money and use it to pay down debt.

I owned two boats. I hated to part with it, but I sold one. The day it drove off I felt like crying, but I used the money to pay off my truck. That rid me of a monthly payment of just over four hundred dollars. I started applying that four hundred to my largest credit card balance every month. It didn't take long to pay off all my balances this way. It snowballed. Every time I paid off a balance it freed up even more money to apply elsewhere. At the beginning of my debt ridding journey I had that four hundred dollar truck payment, plus another six hundred monthly I was paying on credit cards. Once I paid these off I had one thousand extra dollars each month.

If you have a home mortgage, how fast could you pay it off by plopping down an extra grand every month? If you have a mortgage, that's going to be your biggest obstacle. Eventually you will have to sell your home so you can run away and live on a boat. If you've refinanced it several times in order to purchase all your toys, you may be so far underwater you'll never achieve your dream life. You may have some equity in it. Either way, start thinking now about selling your house someday. You're not going to need it anymore.

Let me reiterate. Debt free equals freedom. That's the vital ingredient of the plan. Having zero debt gives you wings to fly. You can live your life as you damn well please.

Quotes from The Way To Wealth,
by Benjamin Franklin

"When you run in debt; you give to another power of your liberty."

"Buy what thou hast no need of, and before long thou shalt sell thy necessaries."

"There are two ways to increase your wealth. Increase your means or decrease your wants."

I chose to decrease my wants, and now I have it all. No, I'm not wealthy in the conventional sense. Most would consider me to be quite poor, but I'm as free as a person can get in this world, and that makes me very rich indeed.

I do whatever I chose and I make no apologies for it. Yesterday I chose to view a spectacular sunrise over Punta Blanca Island. Then I chose to lounge around in my boxer shorts reading a good book all morning. Later I chose to hang out on the beach and play with the manatees. Eventually I opted for a few cold beers as I watched another gorgeous sunset over Cayo Costa.

As I laid my head on the pillow last night, there was nothing to bother my mind. No stress, no worries, it was another carefree day in Paradise. I had no debt, no obligations, nothing but the purest sense of contentment.

8

SAVE, SAVE, SAVE

So I got myself all debt free and I was quite pleased about it. Kim and I had a little mini celebration the day I mailed off the last check. A huge burden had been lifted and we felt a great sense of progress towards our dream. There was just one little problem. We still had no money to finance the dream. I had a few thousand dollars in a checking account. I didn't even have a savings account.

That brings me to step number three. Save money, lots of it, right away. Save money as fast as humanly possible. Once you stop buying stuff, and pay off your debts, saving money becomes easy.

The obvious starting point for me was that extra grand I had each month that used to go to loan payments. I stuck every penny of it into a brand new savings account. That's twelve thousand dollars each year. In five years I could save sixty thousand dollars, more than enough to buy a decent boat. I had the makings of a five year plan without any change at all in spending habits or lifestyle. This was no sacrifice.

I was still going to need money to eat though, and to buy booze. Then it dawned on me that I had quit buying stuff. There ought to be at least a little extra cash in my paycheck each week. I used the direct deposit option offered through my employer and started putting fifty dollars per week into that savings account. It didn't take long to realize that I didn't miss that fifty buck one bit. I then increased my weekly deposit to one hundred dollars. That's five thousand, two hundred dollars a year. In five years that would be another twenty six thousand. Probably not enough, but a good start. I was accumulating cash like I never believed possible and I hadn't given up a single luxury.

I had stopped buying stuff, gotten myself out of debt and money was piling up. Hell if I never quit my job to run away and live on a boat, I was still way better off than I used to be. I could smell the dream though. I could see the sun. I could feel the heat. I could feel my toes in the water and my ass in the sand.

I got so pumped up about the possibility of this crazy dream coming true, I decided to see what affect a little sacrifice would have on the rise of the savings account balance. I started with easy things like a few less nights of eating out. I upped my weekly deposit to one hundred and fifty dollars. With a few more minor adjustments like turning down the thermostat and trying to save a few bucks at the grocery store, I was able to up my deposit to two hundred.

During this period, I learned a little about myself and Americans in general. We've all become so spoiled. We waste so much money, buying whatever suits our fancy whenever we feel the urge. We go to the movies and drop fifty dollars on popcorn and soda. We stop at convenience stores for coffee, or at Starbucks. We eat fast food for lunch and dinner at Applebees. We waste money on trinkets and toys. It's insane really. It really is no mystery why we are all broke and asshole deep in debt.

Somehow, Kim and I broke out of that pattern. With our shared vision of the future constantly in mind we stopped the pointless spending. We learned to enjoy staying home and to enjoy each other. We took pride in our growing savings. We shared our dream. It was like we had a big secret the rest of the world didn't know about.

SAVE, SAVE, SAVE

With further belt tightening and more miserly ways, eventually that deposit grew to three hundred dollars. The savings grew and grew.

How much is enough? I guess that's up to each individual dreamer. If you knew how little money we have to live on, you would most likely call us crazy, but our needs are few. Our debts are none. A recurring bit of advice from fellow cruisers is to go now. Go as soon as you can. They all wish they had started sooner.

One day we decided we had enough. We had enough money and we had taken enough of the work till you die world. Were we absolutely safe and secure with our decision? Of course not, but we took a leap of faith anyway. I wouldn't trade that for the wealth of ten Donald Trumps.

9

LEAP OF FAITH

From The Cape, by Guy Clark

He was eight years old with a flour sack cape

Tied all around his neck.

He climbed up on the garage

Figuring what the heck.

He screwed his courage up so tight

That the whole thing come unwound.

He got a running start and bless his heart

He headed for the ground.

He's one of those who knows that life

LEAP OF FAITH

Is just a Leap of Faith.

Spread your arms and hold your breath

And always trust your cape.

I first heard the song performed by Captain Josh Ramsteck, one of the nicest guys in the Florida music scene. Every time I hear it I'm taken back to when I was a little boy. It's given me great inspiration.

The title of this book is Leap of Faith, but it's also what we chose to name our boat. The whole concept of taking that leap of faith is how Kim and I got to where we are today. Sometimes you just need to jump off that roof because you're pretty sure you can fly.

That certainly applies to how we made our way to Key West for the first time. We had only taken the boat out into the open Gulf of Mexico once, and that did not go so well. We followed some friends out through the Boca Grande Pass, made it six miles out then developed engine trouble.

Dead in the water, we soon found ourselves sideways to big rolling waves. Leap of Faith was rocking violently from side to side as I climbed down into the engine room to address a clogged fuel filter. What was normally a simple task was being made nearly impossible due to the severe pitching back and forth we were experiencing. Things in the cabin started flying around. Our television crashed from its perch above the refrigerator. The hatch I had left open crashed shut and narrowly missed smacking me in the head. I was being tossed about down below, dropping wrenches and banging into bulkheads.

We called to our buddy boat and they threw a line to our bow. Once they pulled our bow into the waves I was finally able to restart the engine. I had no idea that the old Ford Lehman would start while still in gear, but that's what happened. Kim started screaming and I looked up to see our bow about to plow into their stern. We all scrambled for gear shifters and lines like madmen. They got us unattached and themselves moving forward. I got us stopped and the collision was avoided. I'll never forget the looks on their faces and I'm sure glad no one else was around to witness our little nautical circus.

In no mood to continue our planned journey to Fort Myers Beach, we tucked tail and limped back in through the Pass to the safe confines of Pelican Bay.

That was the extent of our offshore experience when I agreed to follow another couple on a trip to the Keys. There I go jumping off the roof again, but they had made the trip before. All I had to do was follow. What could go wrong?

Plans were made and the date was set. We took on what seemed like tons of extra provisions. Just the booze alone settled the boat a few inches deeper in the water. I took extra care with engine maintenance. I changed the oil and replaced fuel filters and loaded up on diesel. We were all set.

The other couple was not. A bad alternator had them stuck at the dock. We were as ready as we could be to get going so we departed Punta Gorda with plans to meet up when they solved their problem. We sat in Pelican Bay waiting. They let me know that they were now also in need of a new voltage regulator and it would be a few more days. Anxious to move on, we motored down the Intercoastal to Fort Myers Beach hoping to rendezvous there. We did, except they came by car. We had a nice dinner at Doc Ford's Rum Bar while they explained their plan to meet up with family in a few days at Marco Island. They thought that now their boat was ready, so once again we set off without them hoping to meet up further south.

We had still not successfully completed an offshore trip. There is no inshore route for a boat our size from Fort Myers Beach to Marco, so this would be our first real test. I set it up with a buddy to receive a text message from me every hour with our GPS coordinates. He was to follow our course using Google Earth. After catching a lovely sunrise over Matanzas Pass, we cruised out from San Carlos Bay into the smooth blue waters of the Gulf of Mexico.

It could not have gone any better. Dolphins played in our bow wake. Flying fish skipped the flat surface of the sea. Just over thirty five nautical miles and six hours later we were entering Factory Bay, Marco Island. We did it! Our first successful offshore trip was cause for another of our mini celebrations.

I let all concerned parties know that we had arrived safely. This was when I learned that our partner boat had yet another problem. The folding prop on their pretty sailboat would not open up. The boat wouldn't move. If we were going to continue to the Keys we were on our own.

Confidence buoyed with a grand total of one offshore cruise under our belt, I sat down with my charts and plotted a course further south. The destination was to be Little Shark River, which turned out to be fifty-eight nautical miles from Marco.

We were already in the Gulf as the sun rose above the eastern horizon. I continued with our locational text messages as we turned south and left Marco Island in our wake. The coastline in this part of Florida is a whole lot of nothing. Traveling south you pass the Ten Thousand Islands on your port side. After that it's all Everglades.

On my fifth text message of the day, my buddy noted that I should be losing sight of land. I answered that he was correct. We were in the middle of nowhere. It was the last message he would get from me for a long time.

Staying well west of the shoals at Cape Romano, we had lost cell phone service. Other than a slight nervousness about being out of touch, our day out in the Gulf was fantastic. The farther south we went, the more clear the water became. It was very calm and still. We could see big schools of tarpon on either side of us. We could not see land but the Gulf seemed like a giant mill pond with hardly a ripple on its surface.

Late in the afternoon as we angled southeast back towards the coast, we could make out the shoreline again. Just as we approached the mouth of the river, an east wind started to build. We got the anchor down in the lee of the tallest mangroves I'd ever seen. We'd been offshore for almost ten hours and out of sight of land for a good part of it. Kim said, "Good job captain." I replied, "Good job mate." Then we both said, "Good job Miss Leap."

Our celebration was cut short by the sight of some angry looking black clouds blossoming up over the mangroves. I double checked our anchor set. We closed up the hatches and prepared to ride out the storm. Soon we took the full brunt of a torrential tropical downpour. Forty mile per hour winds whipped at the canvas on the flybridge. We spent a rocky first night in that primitive wilderness, cut off from the world.

When the deluge let up in the morning, and the winds died down, we stepped out on the deck to survey our surroundings. Instantly we were set upon by the biggest swarm of the meanest mosquitoes this side of the Amazon. We beat a hasty retreat back inside the cabin to slather ourselves in bug spray.

The next hour was spent swatting evil demon bugs all over the ceiling and walls and windows. It was a battle of epic proportions that I can't say we ever won. The inside of the boat looked like a war zone and the best we could do was hold it to a tie. We put duct tape over the gaps in our sliding windows. We sprayed the screens with bug spray. One of us was always on patrol swatting crazily at any stray flying devil we encountered.

This was not paradise at all. We had to get out this Godforsaken swamp. With no cell phone or internet, our only connection with civilization was the VHF weather radio out of Key West. Imagine our disappointment as we listened to a horrible forecast for the Keys. The mechanical voice told us to expect severe storms and strong gusty winds for the next several days all across the lower Keys. There was nothing to do but sit tight.

We were safe in a protected cove. We still had plenty of food, and thankfully plenty of booze. We also had plenty of mosquitoes. After three days suffering through the Everglades version of Amittyville Horror, and no improvement in the forecast, we started to debate what we would run out of first. As the storms came and went we set up to collect rainwater to refill our water tanks. We inventoried the food and booze and decided we were still okay. Then it occurred to us there was one very important item we were low on . . . bug spray.

Also after three days our friends back on land started to worry. We learned later that Facebook was abuzz with concern as to our whereabouts. Eventually the more nervous nellies in the bunch decided to call the Coast Guard. Phones were ringing all over Charlotte County with folks discussing what they knew or didn't know about our trip and where we might be. We were oblivious to all of this of course, busy drinking beer, swatting mosquitoes and joking about malaria.

On day five the storms abated for a few hours. The wind was still blowing fairly strong though, and we were able to enjoy some time outside the cabin without fear of death by bug bite. I struck my favorite pose with my feet propped up on the transom. I had a book in one hand and a beer in the other when Kim said, "Hey look, it's an airplane". We hadn't seen a single plane in five days so I guessed something odd was up. It drew closer and flew a tight circle directly overhead. I looked at Kim and said, "It's a Coast Guard plane". We both looked up and waved. Kim was certain they were there looking for us. I hoped they weren't. She turned out to be right.

On day six our weather cleared a little bit more, but the Keys forecast was still not good. I was able to take the dinghy up the river and chase tarpon, but none of them was willing to cooperate. I saw giant spotted rays and several huge sea turtles. I caught some fat, healthy looking trout and donated some more blood to the flying vampire population. That night listening to the forecast for the fortieth time, I thought Kim was going to cry. The storms over the Keys were moving off but the winds were still way up. Leaving in the morning would be a real gamble considering our meager experience.

We were both beginning to crack, but Kim a little more so. She suggested none too kindly that we just forget it and turn back north. I didn't want to give up yet so I told her we'd see what the morning forecast brought.

LEAP OF FAITH

Before dawn on day seven the now familiar voice from the weather radio told me the storms were gone. He also told me to expect winds from the east at twenty to twenty five knots. I woke Kim and we discussed it. Peering out into the Gulf it didn't look so bad. A bright and clear morning was breaking, along with a crisp breeze. We decided to make a break for it, heading south for Marathon.

Gingerly steering Leap of Faith as close to shore as I dared, I used the tall mangrove trees as a wind break. It was definitely windy, but the seas were doable. I worried what would happen later when first we'd have to skirt the shallows at Cape Sable, then lose our protection as we got south of the mainland. Crossing Florida Bay we would be completely out in the open, with nothing to prevent those winds from churning up bigger waves. Our last two legs had been in fair weather with light winds. Were we ready for rough weather and big seas?

We found out soon enough. Once we left the lee of land, the wind blasted us on our port side. Six foot waves rolled and curled in front of me from left to right. You could surf these waves I thought. Miss Leap bucked and reared like a frightened horse. She refused to steer a straight line as the occasional eight- footer would crest under her bow and shove us off course.

I was wrestling the wheel when we heard the crash from down below. Something had hit hard and shattered. I was still fighting to hold some semblance of a straight course when a second loud bang rang out to us from the cabin below. Kim did not want to climb down the ladder in the tossing seas to see what was going on. She didn't want to take the wheel during the spin cycle of the giant washing machine we were in either. We left the debris to roll around and dug in for the long day ahead.

We plowed and bounced for hours until we could see Vaca Key and the surrounding islands. These keys gave us some measure of protection and the seas became manageable. Relaxing a bit, Kim saw that she now had a cell phone signal for the first time in a week. I dreaded turning mine on, knowing it would be full of texts and voicemails due to our absence. We each had multiple messages from the Coast Guard from both St. Petersburg and Key West. We each had dozens of messages from friends pleading with us to get in touch. I wanted to put off dealing with mine until we were safely moored in Boot Key Harbor, but Kim made the more urgent return calls right away.

It took eight uncomfortable hours before we passed under the Seven Mile Bridge into impossibly dazzling blue waters. It got rough all over again on the Atlantic side so we couldn't relax just yet. I let out a huge sigh of relief when we nosed into Boot Key Channel to pick up a mooring ball. After getting Leap of Faith settled on her mooring, I checked the cabin for damage. The hanging brass lantern above the settee had broken free and lay shattered on the floor. The heavy computer desk had capsized and thrown our laptop over into the galley. Assorted non-breakables were strewn about.

We cleaned up the mess on the floor, then we cleaned up the mess on our phones. I logged in to Facebook to announce our return from the dead and promised more complete updates later. The Coast Guard may have been glad that we were okay, but they seemed annoyed that we wasted their time. We hoped that wouldn't send us a bill.

Checking in with the city of Marathon marina was not what I expected. We had heard that Marathon was very boater friendly and had all the services anyone would need. We found the harbor master and told him which ball we had picked up. He immediately started bitching us out because we didn't call ahead. He would assign us a specific mooring, tell us where we were allowed to tie up. I mentioned the half empty status of his mooring field and Kim schmoozed him up until he agreed to let us stay where we were. Good job captain, good job mate, good job Miss Leap. We were in the Keys.

10

THE KEYS

We spent two days being unimpressed by Marathon. The shower facilities were dungeon-like. Prisons have better bathrooms. The mooring field is between Boot Key and Vaca Key and it's not very scenic. Most of the anchored boats appear derelict. The fee to stay on a mooring ball is twice what we've paid elsewhere. I walked at least a mile to find the Publix grocery store in order to replenish some necessities. The walk back felt twice as long with the load I was carrying. Kim waked the half-mile with me to a liquor store to top off the booze supply. A beggar hit me up in the dayroom. On the plus side we had an awesome breakfast at the Stuffed Pig right across the street and a decent, affordable dinner at Dockside on the other side of the harbor. Two days was enough, so we motored out into Hawk Channel bound for Bahia Honda.

Nice day, pretty water, we were on the move and it felt good. All was well until we entered the Bahia Honda channel. The current was running out of there stronger than any I've ever encountered. I had to push our old engine hard just to make any progress and maintain steerage. We got our anchor down and I was afraid to leave the boat until I was certain it had taken hold in the surging tide.

Bahia Honda is a unique and interesting place. It's between two bridges, and the state has removed a section of the old bridge to allow boats access to the anchorage. It's visually beautiful with one of the better beaches in the Keys. It's a busy place and lots of things happened to us here even though we only stayed one day.

The first thing that happened was we got kicked off the beach! We had landed our dinghy, set up beach chairs and were just relaxing and enjoying the afternoon when a park ranger politely asked us to leave. It seems they don't allow dinghies on the beach. We packed up and found a dock at a store that services the campground and park goers. Inside we found bug spray that contained forty percent DEET. With the memories of Little Shark River still fresh on our minds we snatched up several cans.

We returned to Leap of Faith to see a fifty foot sailboat anchoring uncomfortably close to us. I took the dinghy over to express our concern but the captain blew me off. There were lots of fishing boats coming and going due to a nearby boat ramp. Jet skis buzzing in all directions sent wakes colliding with other wakes. We had that big sailboat up our butt. It all made for a nervous stay, especially with the strong current and questionable holding.

The following morning I was out chasing tarpon again when Kim called me. She was frantic. I zoomed back to the boat. Upon boarding Kim told me that our anchor windlass had started letting out chain all by itself. I checked our position against the too close sailboat and we looked okay, so I went forward to the bow to see a big pile of chain just dumped on deck. After it was all re-stowed in the chain locker I tripped the breaker so it couldn't do it again. That was enough of Bahia Honda.

Back out into Hawk's Channel we went. We made the short hop to Saddlebunch Key. This was an undeveloped, peaceful little spot where we spent a quiet evening away from any excitement. We needed to rest up in preparation for the expected craziness of Key West.

11

KEY WEST

From: Is This The USA?
By Scott Kirby

The customs man met her at the end of the pier

He handed her a shot of tequila and an ice cold beer

Transsexual fire breathing acrobats

Russian jugglers and high flying cats

The customs man said how about that and smiled

She took one long look at the captain

And all she could say

Are you absolutely positive

This is USA?

LEAP OF FAITH

Ah Key West, it's the last resort. It's the end of the line for America's weirdos, renegades and societal dropouts. It's been called an alcoholic theme park in paradise. You've heard it all before in books and songs. It's Ernest Hemingway and Jimmy Buffett rolled into one, then steeped in beer and rum.

It was to be my first visit by land or sea. I didn't really know what to expect, but I was ready. The last destination of our first big cruise was just around the bend. We approached via the main ship channel that the cruise ships use, and it was crazy. Confusing boat traffic and strong current and unfamiliarity conspired to disorient me. Finding a decent spot to anchor was crazy too. Hundreds of vessels from derelict to megayacht crowded every known anchorage. More craziness met us at the dinghy dock in Key West Bight. Floating, half floating, and "how the heck is that still floating" dinghies were tied to every available space. We poked and prodded and managed to squeeze our way in.

As we set foot on dry land we bumped into our cruise partners who weren't. They had made a six hour drive from Punta Gorda to meet us for dinner. I thought that was a bit crazy too, but hey, we took three weeks to get here by boat. We had endured the waiting, the loss of our buddy boat, the uncertain offshore passages, and the diabolical insects of the Everglades. We had persevered through the storms, the winds and the big waves. We had successfully navigated Leap of Faith to new and strange destinations. Now we had arrived at the strangest of them all. We had made it to Key West.

We spent a week in Key Weird. It's got to be the best people watching place ever. We walked Duval Street and the side streets. We hit the majority of the bars. It was surprisingly neat and clean in spite of the drunkenness and debauchery. We went here and there, did this and that, and bought the T-shirts. We watched the sun set from Mallory Square, but it was better from the deck of our boat. We missed the transsexual fire breathing acrobats, but we did see the juggler and high flying cats. Then there was the music. We heard lots of great performers all over town, with a special nod to Michael McCloud at Schooners Wharf.

We also spent lots of money, too much. It was time to make our escape. We had a great time, and everyone should visit at least once, but it was time to go home.

The weather forecast was good for the foreseeable future. I studied the charts and plotted a course directly from Key West to the mainland, skipping the route through Marathon. Obviously my confidence had improved greatly with the sea time we had logged on the way down.

We were already underway when the sun rose over Key West, motoring up the Northwest Channel towards the open waters of the Gulf once again. Midway across we were thirty miles from land in any direction. There were no other boats spotted, just us and the dolphins. It took almost twelve hours to cover the sixty-six miles back to the coast. As we neared the entrance to Little Shark River the weather was still fair with only a slight chop on the sea. I made the decision not to go into the river. We dropped anchor right out there in the Gulf, a mile offshore. I hoped this would save us from the evil, heat seeking mosquitoes that came out of the mangroves at night. That plan didn't work perfectly, but we were prepared with our mosquito defense systems and our forty percent DEET. Other than the bug spray melting Kim's nail polish, we made it through the night without too much damage.

The next few days brought pleasant cruises back north through Marco Island, Fort Myers Beach and eventually home to Pelican Bay. We felt like salty old dogs now. All told we traveled four hundred and eighteen nautical miles. We had expanded our horizons with five weeks living solely at anchor in unfamiliar surroundings. We learned so much about ourselves and our boat. As a couple, we were closer than ever. The experience we gained was invaluable, but best of all it was a grand adventure.

12

SUNSETS

Come late afternoon I joined a lot of other people heading over to Mallory Square to catch the latest edition of the daily sunset. I reckon a lot of them people must not have sunsets where they come from, because it's like the main attraction of the day in Key West.

From Key Weird
By Robert Tacoma

They're saying goodbye, Curtis. Goodbye to the sun, so it will feel needed and return tomorrow. They do it every day. An old custom, from the original Indians they say.

LEAP OF FAITH

"Yes sir." "And Curtis." "Sir?" It's never failed once in all those years . . . ."

From Honorable Mention (The Honor Series)
By Robert N. Macomber

I've always loved a beautiful sunset, even when I lived on land. I've always appreciated them and tried to infect others with the same admiration. Sometimes driving home from work I'd snap a picture with my cell phone and text it to Kim with the message "Sunset for you". Other times we'd be out in the boat and linger a little longer so we could watch it set over the Chesapeake Bay.

The busy life of an average person just doesn't have time to take a minute to appreciate God's beauty, to stop and take a moment to kiss the day goodbye. That's not the case in Key West. They celebrate the sunset like it's New Years Eve, everyday. To a lesser extent that's true for all around Charlotte Harbor as well. We often hear someone blowing a conch shell from their boat here in Pelican Bay. More than once we've listened to a bagpipe rendition of Amazing Grace as that fiery orange ball dipped below the mangroves and sizzled into the Gulf. We even watched a guy bring his guitar out onto his bow and sing When The Sun Goes Down On Charlotte Harbor, a Jim Morris tune.

SUNSETS

There was a party going on one day at The Southbeach Bar and Grill in Boca Grande. Everyone was eating and drinking and the music was playing. With all of the fun being had it got quite loud. Then suddenly there was silence. It was that magical moment when the Sun sits perched on the horizon. Folks drifted down to the beach and no one said a word for five minutes until the Sun winked out and all of its light was gone. Then everyone started clapping, a standing ovation for the Sun.

It remains the central attraction of our day. There are two things we don't miss, happy hour and sunset.

Even if you never quit your job and live on a boat, take a minute. Celebrate the Sun.

13

FRIENDS AND THINGS

From What Kind of Fool Can I Be, by Jim Morris

My friends all think my life's a walk in the park

I write a few lines and I fish until dark

I take time to read and I make time to think

But mostly I just daydream and drink

So what kind of fool can I be?

I live in the sun by the sea

Running around taking life so easily

What kind of fool can I be?

No that song was not written about me, but it's an uncanny depiction of my life. I fish, I read, I daydream and I drink. Throw in a beach and a sunset and you've pretty much got my life covered.

As far as what my friends think, I can't speak for all of them. I hope they are happy for me. Speaking of friends, that's another consideration for you as you plan your getaway. All of the people presently in your life; friends, family and coworkers, they won't be coming with you. I know that sounds hard. Maybe you can't imagine leaving those you care about behind. Kim and I dwelt on this topic several times before we took off.

Look at it like this. Do you still see your high school friends often? College friends, army buddies, ex-girlfriends or boyfriends and former coworkers all come and go. Life moves on and so do you. We always seem to find new friends whenever we move on to a new episode in life.

I was once discussing this very same topic with a wise woman, who happened to be married to my father. I asked her how they could move off to the wilderness of Maine and leave us and all of their friends behind. She told me it was their shared dream to live in a log cabin in the woods, separated from all the dramas normal life brings. It was time to live for themselves, and most of that drama comes from family and friends. She went on to tell me that since they moved away, their relationship was closer and their love deeper than ever before. It was a long time ago but it stuck in my mind.

I had to leave behind the best friend a guy could ever have. We worked side by side for twenty years. We watched each other's children grow up. We stood beside each other through good times and bad. He was my faithful beer drinking buddy, best man in my wedding, and fixer of my broken mechanical things. But, I could be working with him right now, or I could be sitting on the back of my yacht in paradise watching the dolphins go by. I hope he understands.

You probably have a friend or two like that. You could talk to them, share your dream, but they would probably call you crazy.

On the day we arrived in Punta Gorda, we knew a grand total of two people in the town. Now we have so many friends I can't count them. When we were leaving our old life behind we never imagined we'd gain so many great people in our life. The boating community is like that. You can make quick friends with total strangers thanks to obvious shared interests. We were also accepted with open arms by everyone in the music scene around southwest Florida, especially the Parrotheads. Whenever we go ashore, we are happy to see such fine folks and they are happy to see us. It makes having left our old friends just a little bit easier.

Friends aren't the only thing you will be moving on from, which brings me to step four in your plan for ultimate freedom. Get rid of your stuff. That's right, get rid of your stuff, all of it, as fast as you can.

> *"Change is hard because people overestimate the value of what they have – and underestimate the value of what they may gain by giving that up."*

James Belasco and Ralph Stayer, Flight of the Buffalo

> *"It's the preoccupation with possessions, more than anything else, that prevents us from living freely and nobly."*

Bertrand Russell

> *"Unnecessary possessions are unnecessary burdens. If you have them, you have to take care of them! There is great freedom in simplicity of living. It is those who have enough but not too much who are the happiest."*

Peace Pilgrim

So you stopped buying stuff. You paid off your debt. You saved up some cash. Now you need to get rid of all your possessions, not just the toys. Get rid of your tools, your knick-knacks, your vacuum cleaner, your microwave. It's all got to go. Our rule was if it won't fit on a boat it's gone.

Sell things on Craigslist. Have yard sales. It would be nice to make a little more cash to pad your kitty, but the important thing is to lose the stuff. Give it away to friends. Donate it to charity. You have been a slave to your possessions your entire life. Separate your self-worth from the things that you own. You really won't be losing anything, you'll be gaining your freedom.

We started slowly. The easy things to part with went first. I gave Christmas supplies to a friend with a new apartment and no decorations. I opened a coat closet that hadn't been touched in two years. If we hadn't used it in two years we could certainly do without it. I was more willing than Kim in the beginning. She was obviously reluctant to part with her stuff. I didn't push the issue, but trudged on with my own purging of belongings. I took an informal inventory of all the crap we had accumulated. Look around your house, your garage, your attic, your basement. Look at all the stuff! Maybe you even had to buy a shed because you ran out of room in the house. Maybe you rented a storage unit to keep your overflow of stuff.

I had a big garage with no cars in it. There was no room for cars. It was full of tools and toys and more fishing gear than some tackle shops I've been in. I sold four heavy trolling rods at once. Then I sold a few light tackle spinning rods. I picked out a couple of good rod and reel combos to give to my stepson. I also boxed up a bunch of lures and gadgets for his Christmas present. I called over my best fishing partner and let him shop the remainder, keep only a couple rods for myself.

I sold an ice maker, gave away a shop vac and air compressor. I offered other tools to the guys at work. I picked and cleaned and I sold and I gave until the garage was empty. Each item that left took a little weight off my shoulders. I can do this. I was proud of myself, and already starting to feel more freedom.

I turned my attention to selling the other boat that I owned. We both loved that thing. I had bought it cheap, in a sad state. Kim helped me to restore it and we spent many days enjoying her. It had been our getaway from the daily grind. Of all the physical objects I owned, this was the hardest to part with. I put it on Craigslist for a fair price, and it was gone in no time. As she pulled away from the dock that day, with her new owner at the helm, I felt a twinge of sadness. It was for the greater good though. I put the cash in savings and never looked back.

Meanwhile, back in the house, the lovely Miss Kim was slow to get with the program. She had seen all the comings and goings from the garage, but had not gotten into the spirit yet. I took her out there and showed her the big empty space with its floor swept clean. I told her that it felt good to be unburdening myself. A little something clicked that day, but the house was still full.

She went through her clothes little by little until she had a bag full to take to Goodwill. I did the same and the house was lighter by two bags of donated clothing. This went on for months until the folks at two different Goodwill stores knew me by name.

By now, Kim was starting to feel the freedom. Each thing we let go of made us lighter. The place was looking pretty bare and our excitement was building. We made a deal to sell the washer and dryer to the landlord and leave them in place. Then by chance, we met a guy who was living with nothing. He had a cheap apartment with no furniture whatsoever. Jesus said to sell your possessions and give to the poor in order to feel more perfect. In our case we gave our possessions straight to the poor. We offered him a deal. If he would wait until the day we were ready to leave, let us keep our furnishings until the last minute, then he could have it all. He agreed and we were all set.

When the day came he showed up with two trucks, a trailer and some helpers. They proceeded to free us from our furniture and small appliances. Kim dumped the grounds from the coffee pot and handed it to him on his way out the door. I shook crumbs from the toaster and piled it into the back of a truck as they pulled out of the driveway.

Inside we looked around at the emptiness. It was all gone. We had a few duffel bags with clothing. We had our laptop and cell phones. Kim held on to her good Calphalon cookware, and we kept a few photos and momentos we couldn't part with. It all fit in the back of my truck and we were ready to face the unknown.

I have to admit that I felt some conflicting emotions at that moment. Jumping off the garage with nothing but a flour sack cape should make anyone nervous. I was leaving the only life I had ever known and was facing an uncertain future, but I was light in my soul and for the first time ever, I was free.

14

TAKING OFF

"The oldest and strongest of emotion of man-kind is fear, and the oldest and strongest kind of fear is fear of the unknown."

H.P. Lovecraft

"A dream is your creative vision for your life in the future. You must break out of your current comfort zone and become comfortable with the unfamiliar and unknown."

Denis Whitley

"You block your dream when you allow your fear to grow bigger than your faith."

Mary Manin Morrissey

TAKING OFF

Three days after Christmas, with our goodbyes said, we stowed our meager belongings in the truck. We made our way to I-95 and started south. The day before, I had been forced to shovel snow one last time. I had no boots or heavy coat. They had gone to Goodwill. I froze my butt off in a light jacket and deck shoes clearing the sidewalk and driveway, but I was grinning the whole time. Never again, I was thinking.

I wanted to drive south until we could see no more snow on the ground today. That turned out to be the lower part of South Carolina. Along the way we talked about how crazy it was, just ditching it all and driving off in to the unknown. All I knew was that today I had no job to report to, no debts to repay, no one to count on me except Kim, and I was feeling mighty good about it all. What would happen tomorrow? Who knows? We were just at the point where our feet were leaving the roof, no turning back now.

As partners, we had built our dream bigger than our fears. We had stepped away from the mainstream of society and loosed the chains of materialism. There were many doubters, and we proved them all wrong. I had a great boss, and we'd been together many years. Even he didn't really believe I was leaving until very close to the end. I thanked him for all the opportunities he had given me over the years, especially the opportunity to make some nice bonus money, which I promptly spent on boats.

It's impossible to adequately describe how I felt as we continued south on the interstate. We smiled and laughed a lot, kept saying "Can you believe this is really happening?"

At the end of two days on the road we landed in Cocoa Beach. Captain Josh was opening for Jim Morris and the Big Bamboo Band at a big New Years Eve party. It was to be the perfect kick-start to our new life. We stayed the weekend in a hotel on the beach and all throughout our stay we ran into Facebook friends we'd never met in person. We also met lots of other folks that had come up from southwest Florida that would later become part of our circle of friends.

Speaking with Captain Josh and his wife for the first time, he told us how he was following a couple on Facebook who were moving to Florida to live on a boat. He said their names were Kim and Ed. We all had a big laugh when he realized that was us.

15

BOAT SEARCHING

"The person who goes farthest is generally the one who is willing to do and dare. The sure-thing boat never gets far from shore."

Dale Carnegie

"Twenty years from now you be more disappointed by the things you didn't do than by the ones you did do. So throw off the bowlines. Sail away from safe harbor. Catch the trade winds in your sails. Explore. Dream. Discover."

Mark Twain

Finally it was time to make the last leg of our ground journey over to Punta Gorda. The excitement we'd been experiencing tripled as we ticked off the last few miles. We were handed the keys to a waterfront condo minutes after our arrival. We settled in with great relief and immediately turned out attention to boats.

There are two schools of thought when it comes to vessels meant to be lived aboard full-time. There is the sailboat crowd and the powerboat crowd, specifically trawlers. Each have their pros and cons. I have never been a sailor, rarely stepped foot on one, so we were looking for a trawler. The huge advantage of a sailboat is fuel consumption, or lack thereof. If you plan to sail the Caribbean Islands and travel the world, you probably want a sailboat. There are also some who were just born sailors. They wouldn't dream of plying crystal blue waters in a smelly old stinkpot of a powerboat. There is certainly something to be said for the romanticism of gliding through calm seas with nothing but the sound of water passing by your hull.

On the other hand, trawlers have much more space for storage, creature comforts and amenities than sailboats of the same size. They are more house-like and less camper-like than sailboats. Trawlers are just more roomy and comfortable, and that's what we wanted.

We had searched the Mid-Atlantic region with no luck. We found nothing in our price range that really got our blood pumping. Our first thought had been to buy close to home, then take our new boat down the Intercoastal Waterway to Florida.

We did however, find the perfect boat on the internet, and it was in Punta Gorda! I had made arrangements with a broker to see it before we even left Maryland. Now that we were in town, we couldn't wait to check her out. The Yachtworld.com listing had many pictures that depicted a beautiful vessel with all the amenities possible. Imagine our disappointment when we were shown a dirty, beaten boat with all the telltale signs of cosmetic neglect. I assumed the mechanical aspects were equally neglected. This was not anything like what we had seen in the pictures. You could tell she had once been that pretty shipshape vessel shown in the ad, but she hadn't fared well since those pictures were taken. It was heart breaking, but I said no thanks. Our high hopes of a quick purchase and immediate start to our new life on the water were dashed.

Our broker, who turned out to be a really nice guy, said he'd get to work finding more boats for us to look at. Together we scoured Charlotte County. We went north to St. Petersburg. We went south to Fort Myers. I drove to the east coast of Florida to look. We saw a vast assortment of boats but none were quite right.

Either we just plain didn't like them, or they had too much wrong with them. We spent the entire month of January looking at boats every day.

Early in February, frustrated, we took a break from the Great Boat Hunt. I took Kim to Fisherman's Village, which is a tropical mall with several restaurants, and a marina. While Kim looked through the shops I took a stroll down the marina docks. There she was. Floating in slip C-18 was the sweetest, cleanest, prettiest looking classic trawler in all of Florida. She was for sale. I couldn't believe my eyes. I was standing there gawking like some dumb tourist when the owner appeared. "Can I help you," he said. I apologized for the intrusion and told him how much I admired his boat. He said "Come on aboard." He and his wife were both extremely friendly as they led me around a fine vessel that was obviously well taken care of. I assured them I was a serious buyer, but that I needed to come back with my wife, and of course no brokers were present.

We made the arrangements and two days later a crowd came to slip C-18. Their broker, our broker, them, us and my one Punta Gorda pal climbed aboard for a closer inspection. We couldn't really find anything wrong with her. No signs of water damage anywhere in the cabins. The bilge was clean and dry. Everything worked as it should. She had only one shortcoming. We had a list of things that aren't absolutely necessary but would be nice to have. These were a bow thruster, auto-pilot, radar and onboard generator. She had none of them. Even her chartplotter was obsolete. She was in so much better condition than anything else we had seen though. Even without the extras, we both loved her. We could do without them. This was our boat.

After completion of a professional survey, we negotiated the price. By mid-February she was ours. We were the proud owners of a 1980 Blue Seas yacht. She was thirty-six foot in length and Europa styled. We moved aboard her full-time on the first of March.

16

MAIDEN VOYAGE

Mighty Neptune, King of all that moves in or on the waves, and mighty Aeolus, guardian of the winds and all that blow before them: We offer our thanks for the protection you have afforded this vessel in the past, but now we submit this application. That the name by which this vessel has previously been known, Norvic, be struck and removed from your records.

In consequence whereof, and in good faith, we seal this pact with a libation offered according to the hallowed ritual of the Sea.

Oh might and great ruler of the seas and oceans, to whom all ships and we who venture upon your vast domain are required to pay homage, implore you in

your graciousness to take unto your records, and rec-
ollections, this worthy vessel hereafter and for all
time known as Leap of Faith, guarding her with your
mighty arm and trident and ensuring her of safe pas-
sage throughout her journeys.

In honor of your greatness, we offer these libations to
your majesty and your court. I offer a toast. To Leap
of Faith and the union of Ed and Kim; may they enjoy
calm seas and gentle winds.

The renaming ceremony was a great excuse for a party.
We invited all of our marina neighbors for the event.
After lubing them up with cheap champagne we made
a bunch of new friends real fast. Boat people will drink
anything, especially if it's free. We had made the boat
ours, and made new friends. We were well on our way
to a cool new life. It was time for our maiden voyage.

It was a calm, sunny blue-sky day when we eased out
of the slip for the first time. I was at the helm for the
first time and nervous as a teenager asking a pretty
girl for a date. I slowly nosed Leap of Faith out into
Charlotte Harbor and began acquainting myself with
the feel of her. I listened closely to the sound of the old
Ford Lehman diesel and tried to figure out the crap-
py little chartplotter. I was trying to steer a wide slow
curve around Punta Gorda, which means Fat Point in
Spanish, but I was having some trouble. The steering

had become loose and sloppy. The farther we went the worse it got, so I stopped. We floated a bit, ate some sandwiches and decided to head back in. By the time we approached the marina entrance I was really fighting the wheel. It took about thirty complete turns of the wheel to make a right into the marina. I spun it back the other way about forty times to turn left along D dock. Nearing C dock I thought she would never turn, but after about fifty or so spins of the wheel she slowly came around. My knuckles were white and I was dripping sweat on the controls. Looking up to locate the slip I saw another boat coming straight at our bow. It was a hundred feet ahead as I slammed into reverse. When I came to a stop we were close enough to chat. He wanted me to go around. I yelled over that I had steering problems and couldn't make it around him safely. We jockeyed around some until I managed to back up enough to allow him to pass in front of me. Me earlier nervousness had grown to near hysteria. A fancy marina full of expensive boats is no time for a new captain to lose his steering. Our confrontation with the other boat had gotten the attention of everyone in the marina. They all knew this was our first time out of the slip and probably thought we were about to provide them with some entertainment. I could feel the pressure of eyes upon me. I was unfamiliar with the boat, had never pulled in to this slip, and I was losing control of her movements. I couldn't just sit there, so I put her in gear and eased forward. One of the marina employees and several neighbors were on the dock with our lines. They were there to help but all I could think of was that they would see how badly I screwed this up.

The time came to turn and I started spinning the wheel like a mad man, forty, fifty, sixty revolutions. "Turn damn it", I muttered under my breath. She started nosing around to port, but not far enough. Seventy, eighty, she's coming around. I almost had it lined up but needed the rudder back the other way to straighten it out. Whipping the wheel back I talked to Miss Leap. "Don't hit the dock baby, don't hit the dock." I got the rudder straight, slide her into reverse to slow down, glided dead center in the slip and brought her to a stop just as sweet as could be. The dockhand said, "Good job Ed." I was so relieved I wanted to raise my arms in triumph and jump up and down. Instead I tried to act like it was no big deal. When things settled down I went about determining just what was wrong.

Turns out the previous owner had neglected to mention a very leaky hydraulic system that controls the steering. Our surveyor didn't find it either. I replaced seals at both the upper and lower helms and tightened a loose fitting down below. It was still leaking somewhere. I hired a mechanic and he rebuilt the cylinder that actually moves the rudder. Three hundred dollars later the problem was solved.

That was my initiation in owning a live-aboard boat, especially an old boat. Things break. Things wear out. Wires corrode, bolts rust and hoses split. Things that move stop moving and things that are supposed to stay still come loose. It really helps if you are at least somewhat handy. Since that day I've spent nine hundred dollars on a new heat exchanger, which I replaced myself. The new starter I installed cost two hundred. The batteries set me back eight hundred. Our refrigerator failed in Key West and that reduced the kitty by fourteen hundred. Filter changes, blown fuses, rewired pumps, failed impellers, there's almost always something to fix. But hey, you'll have plenty of time on your hands once you quit your job and live on a boat.

17

A DIFFERENT WAY OF LIFE

Mechanical breakdowns and boat maintenance are very big parts of the life. There are other aspects of living aboard that will seem, at first, to be major inconveniences. Living at anchor presents several challenges that dirt dwelling folks don't even think about.

There is no cable television. Can you imagine? The trash man doesn't show up once a week to take our garbage. We have no washer and dryer. I often carry five gallon water jugs to shore in order to have water for showers, washing dishes and flushing the head. Sometimes we catch rain water to fill our water tanks. We have warmed water in the sun in order to bathe. We have warmed water on the stove on cloudy days. During the summer months we enjoy cool showers.

None of this may seem acceptable to a person living in normal society. You take them all for granted. To us, it's just part of our normal routine and a tiny price to pay for our freedom. We've learned to manage with what we have. We cope with the challenges by treating them as our adventure for the day.

Trash we hold onto until we get to a place that will accept it. Paying the fee at a mooring field let's you get rid of the garbage. We've done this in Punta Gorda, Fort Myers Beach, and Marathon. You can also dispose of trash from your vessel in Key West. That fee usually gives you access to laundry facilities as well, but we have occasionally taken the dinghy ashore then hauled it a few blocks to a Laundromat. We also use a wash tub and do laundry by hand sometimes.

When I had a job, a house, and a busy, normal life I wouldn't have dreamed of walking two miles round trip for some groceries. I never would have walked a mile to the liquor store, done laundry by hand, caught rain water for personal use, etc. I never thought I'd drive a dinghy that far to buy a Key Lime pie from Topps Supermarket either. It's just a different life. Most of the time at anchor, if we run out of milk or bread or whatever, that's just too bad. There is no convenience store, no grocery, and certainly no Walmart. Out here we simply take whatever comes with a smile. It's all part of the adventure.

There is one more thing that has a huge bearing on everything we do and we have absolutely no control over it. I'm talking about the weather. Now one of the reasons we chose southwest Florida as a place to live is that this area has possibly the finest weather in the continental United States. Still, we pay attention to it daily. Are we going to the beach? Might it rain later? Do we need to shut the hatches? Are strong winds expected? Where should we anchor for the most protection? If we are traveling we consider not just the current weather here, but the forecast for our destination. Is it too windy to go offshore? Is it too windy to go at all?

You've already read about us being stuck in the Everglades due to bad weather. There have been other times when weather ruined our plans, either because it would be too uncomfortable or it was downright dangerous.

Once we ordered tickets online to see our favorite band at the Punta Gorda Jazz Festival. The day before the show we motored twenty miles up Charlotte Harbor and dropped anchor just off one of the towns beautiful parks. The next day we awoke to thirty knot winds and big waves. It rained off and on all day. The show was outdoors and it was not a pretty day.

The seas built even more by show time and we decided not to risk a treacherous dinghy ride in nasty weather.

We missed the show, which went on despite the wind and rain. Now we rarely make advance plans like that, especially if it means spending money on something we might miss due to weather.

We've been forced to skip several social events. We've holed up in the salon of the boat just watching it rain. We've rocked and rolled in unprotected harbors. The weather rules our whims. Thankfully, most of the time, the weather is just plain nice.

Sometimes though, it can get downright mean. One morning at five a.m. we were both jolted awake by a roaring wind like we'd never before heard. It was pitch black dark and hammering sheets of rain poured over the decks. I tried to peak out to locate the source of the noise but it was just too dark. I managed to pick out a few lights onshore and I kept staring at them to make sure we weren't dragging our anchor. Satisfied we weren't moving, and with the ungodly roar subsiding we tried to go back to sleep. The winds were still up, just less noisy. The violent motion of the boat in the washing machine seas kept me awake so I turned on the laptop. My hear skipped a beat when I learned a tornado has just passed by us and touched down a mile away. "That explains the noise," I thought. "Holy Crap", we dodged a bullet that time.

A DIFFERENT WAY OF LIFE

We've also battened down for tropical storm Debbie, which was never dangerous but it rained for five days straight. We seriously prepared for alleged hurricane Isaac, which didn't amount to anything. Hurricanes you say? The number one most asked question I get is "What do you do all day?" Number two is "What about hurricanes?" I did some research before we moved here. Charlotte Harbor has experienced exactly one direct hit from a major hurricane in seventy-five years. Before Charlie devastated Port Charlotte and Punta Gorda, it had been sixty-five years since the last major storm. Hurricanes are more frequent in the Mid-Atlantic.

Back in Maryland, my home was flooded by hurricane Floyd. A few years later Irene flooded large portions of Maryland's Eastern Shore. I decided that southwest Florida is not a hurricane magnet, and is even less prone to direct hits than the Chesapeake Bay area.

We do have the option to have the boat hauled out and tied down if we're likely to get hit. We can also borrow a dock in a canal or run up the Peace River to hole up. So, although weather in general is a constant concern, worrying about a hurricane is a tiny piece of it.

I hope this chapter hasn't scared anyone off. I dreaded writing it, but wanted to be honest with you. Not every single day is sunshine and sandy beaches. I must tell you though, the past few days I've been writing in my beach chair. I take my big old yellow pad onto the white sand of Cayo Costa, peer over it to the blue waters, and hear the soft murmurs of a calm Gulf. It's not exactly miserable.

18

RELATIONSHIPS

"She said, it'll work out. I have no regrets.

You gave me a life that I'll never forget.

She said, I'll be there till the light

Dies in your eyes."

From Tarpon Jim, by Jim Morris

We worked that last line into our wedding vows. I'm bringing it up now because I want to write about relationships. I'm far from a relationship expert, but I do know this. It's extremely important that both spouses, or significant other, totally buy in to the dream. If one of you goes into this venture half-heartedly, it's destined to fail. It's also vital that the relationship is strong and healthy. If you often feel like shooting each other, you'll still want to shoot each other living on a boat, even if it is in paradise. Living as a couple on a boat requires an increased level of harmony and cooperation. That vision that you'll need to share equally also means that you will share a very small space, twenty four hours a day, seven days a week.

Kim and I had a great marriage before moving on to the boat, but thinking back we really didn't spend that much time together. Between our jobs, friends, kids and social engagements, there just was not that much time left for us to be alone together. Those few hours we did have were generally spent sitting in front of the television. We were certainly in love and happy together, but there are a lot of distractions in normal society. These days we rarely leave each other's side. We do most everything together. I no longer play cards with the guys on Friday nights. I'm not at my job for ten hours a day. We are together, all of the time. Our home is a twelve by thirty-six foot space. What has that done for our relationship? We are closer and more loving than ever. I love my wife. I probably would have never made this dream come true without her. Her contributions, her inspiration, and her total willingness to take that leap of faith with me made it all possible.

There are certain challenges that come with this lifestyle that could stress a weaker marriage to the breaking point. There is zero privacy aboard a small boat. No fart or snore goes unheard. No odor goes unsmelled. Your bathroom will be tiny and all manner of intimate items will be comingled in whatever small space is available. Tolerance of each other's quirks and habits is absolutely essential.

There is no place to retreat to in the event of an argument. You are stuck with each other, in good and bad. You are an inseparable team in all that you do.

Just getting started with the planning takes equal commitment from both partners. You both have to stop the spending. I'm not just talking about women here either. I know several husbands who outspend their wives. You have to work together to pay off your debt. You both have to give up the toys. You both have to get rid of your stuff. You will both have to accept a more minimalistic existence. Both partners will need to equally seek out a more simplistic way of life, together as one. You will have to do these things without regrets. Me?

I've got egrets, and no regrets

I've got no money but I've got no debts

And every day I get a free sunset

I've got egrets, and no regrets

LEAP OF FAITH

I aint worried bout anything passing me by

I ain't worried I got all I need

A pretty beach and a sunny sky

I've got egrets, and no regrets

By Jim Morris

19

THE BOATING FRATERNITY

Just because we are always together, doesn't mean we are always alone. We meet lots of people. The boating community is a very friendly and open group. Right away you have common interests. We've found that people who live on boats, whether in a marina or at anchor, tend to develop close friendships much quicker and easier than those living on land.

Of course, some of those acquaintances we make are temporary. Sometimes you'll share a sunset cocktail with cruisers who are just passing through. We shared a nice afternoon with a sail maker in Marathon, even though we may never see him again. He turned us on to the Jack Reacher novels and we've had many hours of enjoyment from them. There was a homeless guy in a park I paid forty dollars to scrape barnacles off my dinghy. I met JR in Charlotte Harbor. He told a great story about fleeing Key West, and his addictions, in a twenty-six foot sailboat. He was anchored not far from an old country songwriter who helped make George Jones famous. This eccentric fellow wore a gold chain with a diamond studded letter E that he swore he got from Elvis.

We spent two evenings drinking beer on a sand spit with a completely hairless gentlemen. His shaved and waxed skin reflected the setting sun as he took off his sarong to reveal a skimpy thong. His bald head and gold earrings made him look a lot like Mr. Clean, only less masculine.

Just recently, a couple approached us on their dinghy and said they had seen us somewhere before. Turns out we had spoken briefly in Key West, a hundred and thirty-five miles south of here.

There are a few regulars that frequent Pelican Bay. We know them by their boat names mostly; War Department, and Fancy Free for example. We even ran into another boat named Leap of Faith once, down in Marathon.

THE BOATING FRATERNITY

You never know who you're going to meet out on the water. We've learned to keep an open mind and not be quick to judge new people. After all we are kindred spirits.

Marinas are a fantastic place to meet new people. We became a family in no time at all with our slip neighbors. Maybe it's living in Florida, but the diversity among people who live on boats is amazing. There's the super friendly couple who travel North America for their job. They have no house, but stay on their forty foot motor sailor when not on the road. There's the older couple living on their cluttered houseboat that's so full of potted plants, decorations and just plain junk it look like it may sink at any minute. That old tub hasn't run in years and never will again. There's the hermit-like fellow that rarely sticks his head up out of the cabin of his pristine Island Packet sailboat. A few slips down lives the younger couple who quit the restaurant business and brought their thirty-two foot Westsail down the river system from Kentucky. She's now a school teacher and he cleans pools. Across from them is the ninety-five year old fellow still living aboard his huge trawler. Every afternoon you can see him napping on the back deck.

There are a few weekenders you get to know, and there are a few absentee owners. You know their boat but you never see the people. Mostly though, marinas make their money off the snowbirds. Those folks who spend summers someplace up north and winters in Florida start filling up the marinas in the Fall.

All winter long the marina is a busy place, bustling with activity and social gatherings. From the cookouts to the sunset parties to the swimming pool, you can't help but make tons of friends.

We get to know so many people and we count them as friends even though they are only here half the year. We drank a lot of booze with a nice couple from New York. They are both retired auto workers who live aboard fulltime. They take their trawler up and down the coast. We got to be close with the sweet nurse who spends her summers in Michigan. Her little sailboat is the prettiest thing, just like her. Her husband is a high powered accountant and has never been anything but nice. Also nice was the couple next to us on the thirty-two foot Carver. He was always flying off on business and generally busy. His wife was very kind to Kim.

At the beginning of C dock is the big mustached guy on his little Pacific Seacraft sailboat. He comes down from Vermont or New Hampshire each winter and rows all over the harbor in his dinghy named S. S. Bailout. He's always upbeat and fun to be around. Down from his is the still spry seventy year old Canadian couple. They are always riding bikes and swimming in the pool.

THE BOATING FRATERNITY

They are neighbors to another spritely couple who are always riding foot powered scooters up and down the dock.

Near them is the mid-seventy year old deckhand. He's still in good shape, still working the fuel dock. Sailed here from middle America someplace thirty years ago on his way to the Caribbean. This is as far as he got. We still see him sometimes at the bar.

We are still friends with all of these fine folks, including the couple from Colorado that can drink with the best of them. I've never been around him when he hasn't offered me a beer. I'll never forget the time we got them good and liquored up aboard our boat and he fell overboard trying to dinghy back to his boat. His wife is the life of the party whenever she's around.

We've met so many people since moving aboard I can't begin to count them all. Some have come and gone. Some are now our closest friends. We're all so different. We are from different places, different social and economic classes, and even different types of boats, but we all come together as part of the boating fraternity.

20

IT'S A CRAZY WORLD

All these interesting characters play the roles that help make this new episode of our lives so fulfilling. In order to get here, we had to run away from the previous episode. What are we running away from and what are we running to?

Way back on September 11, 1964, Paul Harvey wrote an editorial entitled "America Has Become A Society Of Cannibals". He bemoaned the ever enlarging bureaucracy, insidiously reaching farther into our lives and nibbling away at our freedoms. He railed against nanny state regulations and the growth of dependency due to the welfare state. Almost fifty years ago, one of the most astute observers of American culture warned us of what was to come. Within that article he said,

"Already many American industrialists are turning over the keys to their corporations and going to Florida — either part-time or full-time — to become nonproductive beachcombers."

That's just what I did. Beachcombing is one of my favorite pastimes these days. It's not quite up there with drinking beer, but it's close. It certainly beats the Hell out of maximizing profits for a utility company. I use to get paid good money to put up with constant bullshit. Now I'm tickled when I find a sand dollar.

When I started out in my career, I got things done. I grew the business. I satisfied the customers. My team and I came up with new innovations. I took some risks now and then. I spent my energies making sure my people had the proper resources to do the best job possible. I got right down in the trenches with them quite often. I fixed processes, improved efficiency and solved problems quickly. I hired and fired at my discretion. I earned a reputation as a guy who made things happen, got the job done.

Then things started to change. It happened over time but everything got harder. By the end I was a completely different type of manager. I now spent most of my time trying to stay out of trouble with the company bureaucrats. I used up way to much energy attempting to comply with endless regulations. I learned more about

DOT, OSHA, Sarbanes-Oxley and Human Resources than anyone should ever have to know. I covered my ass and kept my head down.

To hire one new truck driver, which could take up to two months time, I'd have a personnel file with forty separate pieces of paper in it. Drug test, criminal background check, high school diploma, security clearance from Homeland Security, you name it. I once had a guy apply who was retired Air Force. He already had a federal government security clearance from when he used to refuel Air Force One at Andrews Air Force Base. My Human Resource department held up his hire because someone else with the same name from a different state had a criminal record. Applicants for customer service were turned down due to poor credit reports.

I had a longtime employee who simply lost his mind. He admitted to me he was seeing a psychiatrist who had prescribed anti-psychotic drugs. He called them his crazy pills. His behavior was extremely erratic so I brought his condition to the attention of our Human Resources department. I offered that since he was a driver hauling hazardous materials, extremely flammable and explosive material, that maybe we should do something. One week later with a doctor's note and the full blessing of the brilliant bureaucrats, he was back on the job. Within days I'm accused by this mentally unstable individual of assaulting him physically. The accusation was completely absurd, but said bureaucrats, terrified of going to court, offered the lunatic a settlement. My character was impeached. I was never given the opportunity to defend myself. I got to keep my job, after a stern rebuke, but I will never forgive those spineless and cowardly company executives who failed to stand up for what was right.

I am but one small example in a world run amok. Political correctness, over-regulation, over-litigation, close to fifty percent of our citizens on some form of government assistance, terrorism, violence, society is in chaos.

The constant barrage of sensory input has us all walking around like zombies, cell phone to our ear. Twenty-four hour cable news bombards us with suicide bombers and IEDs. Young folks occupy and old folks wonder why. Save Social Security. Don't touch my Medicare. Tax the rich. Help the poor. Feed the hungry. Fight obesity.

Inflation, deflation, stagflation, what's a dollar worth? Interest rates are low, refinance now. The stock market is up. The stock market is down. Wall Street is evil. The space shuttle is grounded. Rover lands on Mars. The Fed isn't printing money, It's "Quantative Easing". California is bankrupt. America is broke, but it's okay because we can buy our own debt with money borrowed from China.

How is that Arab Spring working out? Syria kills its citizens. Lybia is aflame. The Muslim Brotherhood runs Egypt. How would you like to be an embassy guard in Yemen? Iran wants a nuke. Israel wants to be left alone. The European Union is more broke than we are. Some guy in Arizona pushes a button and a drone vaporizes a camel in Pakistan. The war in Iraq winds down while the war in Afghanistan drags on. Support our troops. Cut defense spending.

More money for education, school vouchers, charter schools, Department of Education, nationalize student loans, meanwhile we get dumber by the generation.

Super strict gun laws in Chicago result in daily deaths by gunshot. Detroit deemed to dangerous to visit. Camden, New Jersey lays off its entire police force.

Id required for over the counter cold medicine, but not to vote. Illegal immigrant is now undocumented worker. Glen Beck warns of the coming apocalypse. Chris Mathews has a tingle up his leg. Healthcare is a civil right. Down with Obamacare. New Black Panthers coming to a polling place near you. The Justice Department investigates itself, finds itself innocent. Guns to Mexican drug cartels, border agent dead, nothing to see here. Miley Cyrus got a new haircut.

Taxmaggedon is coming. Raise the debt ceiling. GM equals Government Motors. Osama Bin Laden is dead. You didn't build that. Pay for my contraception. We want abortion on demand. Abortion is murder.

Coming up next on American Idol, Pants on the Ground versus She Thinks My Tractor's sexy. Don't miss the next episode of Deadliest Catch, when Kim Kardashian dates an Alaskan crab fisherman. This week's episode of Celebrity Boxing pits Mariah Carey against Nikki Manaj. You know they only kept voting for Bristol Palin on Dancing With The Stars because she's a Republican. Lindsay Lohan is drunk again. I heard her mom does cocaine. Hulk Hogan has a sex tape? Beyonce and Jay Z sure do love Obama. Clint Eastwood talks to an empty chair. Sorry I can't, Survivor is on tonight. Just Tivo it. You can record four shows at once with Century Link. I have to stand in line all night to get my new Iphone 5.

Wendy's has the fastest fast food. It's also hot and juicy. Burger King says have it your way, but McDonalds has better toys in the kid's meal. Which do you prefer, Applebees, Ruby Tuesdays, Olive Garden or TGI Fridays? Your town probably has them all. Your local Super Walmart has a McDonalds inside, in case you have a Big Mac attack while shopping. I wonder why so many best-selling books are about losing weight?

Don't be caught dead in yesterday's fashions. Turn your hat around boy, and pull your pants up. The newest Nikes cost how much? Rent a limo for the prom. Take spring break in Cancun. Tanning beds cause cancer. We tax tanning beds. In order to escape reality, we watch reality shows. Click here to see Kate Middleton's boobs. Make sure your anti-virus is up to date. Is Kate Upton too fat? Is Kate Moss to skinny?

How about those Yankees? Roll Tide. Tim Tebow is a Christian and proud of it. That ugly business at Penn State sure was awful. So was the big wreck at Talladega. The Stones are making a comeback, again. I saw their farewell tour in 1980.

April 15 is tax day. Don't forget your state tax, county tax, local tax, property tax, sales tax, cigarette tax, gasoline tax, death tax, ammunition tax, sugary drink tax and no Big Gulp for you. They taxed me for a bag of ice at the 7-11 last week. Ice is taxable? I guess once you get to tax tanning anything goes. Let's not overlook those hidden taxes. Take a look at your cell phone bill. I especially like that charge that goes to buy free phones for inner-city do-nothings. Years ago we started charging a regulatory compliance fee on your propane delivery. Later we added a fuel charge. Hey it costs lots of money to comply with today's myriad of regulations, and fuel is expensive. Consumers get to pay for that. We must keep our profits up and our shareholders happy.

The IRS is targeting conservative groups. The Department of Justice is tapping the phones of journalists. The National Security Administration is collecting information on the phone calls, text messages, emails and computer usage of millions of Americans. The Youtube video caused Benghazi.

Did you ever feel like you were standing in the middle of a tornado that was filled with flying debris? At any minute you could get clobbered by a Kia Sportage, or smothered by a Serta Perfect Sleeper, or tangled up with a Lybian rebel still clinging to his RPG. One man's terrorist is another man's freedom fighter. If you stop to think about it for a few minutes, you can't help but conclude that the modern world has gone completely insane. Face it. Global conditions are one big chaotic swirling minefield threatening to tear through our trailer park. Meanwhile we consider which new golden gadget to buy while our government prints more money and adds another piece to the gigantic Rube Goldberg regulatory apparatus.

What does it all mean? What do we care? Our young people are obsessed with texting and tattoos. Cuban youth board rickety rafts you wouldn't float in your swimming pool, hoping to cross the Florida Straits and touch American soil before being intercepted by the Coast Guard.

Top professional athletes are now signing contracts that approach one hundred million dollars. We could feed nations of hungry with filet mignon for that kind of money. Al Gore tells us we should buy a Honda Prius in order to do our part for the environment. Meanwhile his electric bill is more than we earn in a month and China is belching black smog pollution faster than your hybrid runs.

We sit in our beautiful homes, surrounded by every luxury and convenience known to man. We eat pizza from Dominos while a government drone watches us tune in to NCIS every Tuesday night at eight. You can't pee on that tree in the backyard anymore, for fear of it showing up on Google Earth.

What does it all mean? What do we care? Snooki is famous. Pause for effect . . . we know her but not our senators or representatives. We're arguing with our GPS in our cars while the United Nations argues about what to do with Iran and Syria. We can't decide where to go to dinner while our Congress can't decide what to do about our debt.

It's all quite maddening. We don't want to think about it. None of it makes sense to us and there's nothing we can do about it. We'll just shut the door, turn on the television, look around at our possessions and block it all out. Sometimes, some of us fantasize about running away. It's a fantasy that has become more and more popular as the world has gotten crazier. Thatched huts on the beach and log cabins in the woods populate the thoughts of daydreamers all across America. That's not a bad thing. You need a dream to run to even more than a past to run away from. If you only want to give up, chuck it all and run away, you can live under a bridge or in a cardboard box. I suspect that attitude makes up a good portion of our homeless. No, you need a dream to run to.

21

LIVING THE DREAM

For me, obviously, the dream was to live on a boat in paradise. It's more than that though. It's the freedom that this lifestyle provides. It's the freedom that comes from knowing that today I can do anything I choose. I am free to enjoy the beauty that nature provides.

Maybe I'll stalk the worlds most sought after game fish, the mighty tarpon. I feel the quiver in my knees as a school approaches, black backs and silvery sides slicing the surface of the azure Gulf. I try to make the perfect cast, presenting my lure expertly, hoping they are willing to play today. My arms are jolted from the lightning strike as the Silver King rises, exploding out the tropical waters in a writhing mass of acrobatic fury. It is primitive raw power combined with grace and beauty. Time slows and I am spellbound as his twisting arc continues impossibly high. Small rainbows form in the shaken off seawater. At the peak of this majestic leap, one more wrenching flip and my lure is dislodged and spit back in my direction. The King crashes down with an ear cracking splash. I glimpse one mirror-like eye as he departs. I imagine him saying "Not today my friend, not today." My heart is beating so fast I can barely retrieve my line. I bow to the King, tip my rod in salute and say "May we meet again, some other day." It's a once in a lifetime experience for many, but I am free to attempt to recreate it anytime I wish.

We may decide to take the dinghy out. We idle around, avoiding the grass beds and shallow flats near the southern end of Pelican Bay. Entering open waters we turn west, now skimming across the surface with the wind in our hair. We pass Primo Island and enter Murdoch Bayou, slowing down to watch for manatees. Then we land the small boat and walk across the island. First we take the path through the mangroves, squishy muck under our flip flops. The earth firms up as we duck under the sea grapes. We sidestep a cactus in the clearing, looking up at the palms in the center of the island. They appear a bit weather beaten, but still stand tall against the cloud-proof sky. Eventually we come to sea grass. Brushing it aside we emerge from the undergrowth and step out onto the talcum powder that we call Sand Dollar Beach.

The first thing we notice is the Gulf. When the light is right, it appears as a salty margarita being gently swirled in a giant glass. When it's calm and cloudless it appears more blue, reflecting the sapphire southwest Florida sky.

We look to the north and see no people. We gaze to the south and there is no one for miles. It's our beach. There is no boardwalk or strip. There are no bars, t-shirt shops, high rise hotels or condos. There is nothing yet there is everything. There is peace and there is freedom. There is a tangy smell of salt air and sea life. Warm plush sand cushions our now bare feet.

We find a sea turtle nest high in the dunes, mother's tracks leading back to sea. We walk among the shorebirds, sharing the surf as they peck the sand for periwinkles. Huge brown pelicans dive bomb a bait pod just beyond the sand bar. The receding tide exposes hundreds of live conchs, burrowing in to await the water's return. Snook glide stealthily along the first drop off, waiting to ambush prey.

The October sun is still warm but pleasant on our skin. Kim's long tan legs contrast against the cottony whiteness of the sand. We are king and queen of the island. Our court is the blue-green sea, the powder puff sand, and the gently swaying palms.

LIVING THE DREAM

The outside world does not intrude upon this coastal Eden. There are no politics here, no rat race to run. There is nothing to be bought and the only show to watch is the ever changing panorama of God's beauty. We have the freedom to share this special place, every single day.

Some days we share a certain kind of laziness and the freedom to do nothing at all. That usually means lounging around the boat with our noses in a book. I'll nap away the afternoon, resting up for happy hour. Kim will doze in the shade on the settee, book in her lap and eyes half open. The lullaby for our siesta is the lapping of waves on the hull and the complaining cry of gulls overhead.

Other times we visit our blubbery friends in Manatee Cove. There are always some of the gentle marine giants there. They are always friendly and willing to pose for pictures. Or we may float with the dolphins, or run to Cabbage Key for a beer. Maybe we'll meet some new friends on the sand spit at Pelican Pass. The choice is ours. We are free.

22

YOUR WORLD VERSUS MINE

Let's compare those last two chapters, your world versus mine. Your world is run by a gridlocked government and a political situation that makes no sense to any rational person. Fiscal cliff flirting politicians have very little effect on my world. I no longer pay federal income tax. Faceless, nameless bureaucrats are no longer using my money for useless studies, foreign aid or causes I don't support.

Terrorism is still a very real threat that we all tend to ignore. Where do you live? Is it within the fallout zone of a major city or military installation? What if terrorists were to strike your favorite shopping mall or your children's school? I'm betting that any destructive act by terrorists won't be directed at an uninhabited coastal island in southwest Florida.

What about economic collapse or civil unrest? The possibility is out there. We have Doomsday Preppers who thinks it's inevitable. I hear they have their own reality show. I'm not one of them, but I'm in a much better position to survive a breakdown of society than the average American family.

What about foreign affairs? What if Iran uses a nuclear weapon? What if Israel goes to war? What if Syria uses chemical weapons? What if a radical Islamist government of Egypt runs amok? There are too many worldwide threats to the fragile American notion of safety for us to comprehend. I feel somewhat isolated from it all in my island paradise.

What if nothing happens? Let's assume our economy survives our own best efforts to crush it. Our government goes on accumulating unfathomable debt and the bill never comes due. The Middle East goes on posturing but never breaks out into all out war. Terrorists never gather the gumption to strike us again. The world keeps turning and tomorrow is just like today.

You'll wake up to the ringing or buzzing of an alarm clock. I don't own an alarm clock. You'll rush for a cup of coffee as you prepare for work. I'll take mine out on deck to watch the sunrise. While you are commuting to a job you don't really like, I'll decide between going fishing or reading a good book. Your afternoons will be spent behind a desk, handling difficult customers, trying to please the boss or meet a deadline. You will be working for The Man so he can make a profit. You will be working for a paycheck so you can pay the bills. You'll be doing all sorts of things you'd rather not be doing. They don't call it work because it's fun.

While you are riding home in the car, bus or train, I'll be piloting my dinghy back to my yacht. You've got to get home to fix dinner or mow the lawn. I've got to get back in time for happy hour. You'll settle in to watch American Idol while I put my feet up to watch another stunning sunset. When we finally lay down our heads, you'll be worrying about the mortgage or what needs to be done at work tomorrow. I won't have a care in the world. Maybe you'll dream of a vacation to someplace warm where you can just get away from it all. You could escape for just one week. I've made my escape permanently.

You live in a commercialized world driven by consumerism and the need to accumulate possessions. I already have everything I really need.

YOUR WORLD VERSUS MINE

"When you are discontent, you always want more, more, more. Your desire can never be satisfied. But when you practice contentment, you can say to yourself, 'Oh – yes – I already have everything that I really need."

Dalai Lama

In your world nothing is ever enough. You long for a better paying job, a newer car, or a bigger house. I am content with what I have. You live in a chaotic, sometimes dangerous world. It simply doesn't reach me here. Your life is an endless routine of work, bills, obligations and commitment. You find your pleasures along the way, but what does it all mean? To what end do you toil?

My only real obligations are to love and care for my wife and my vessel. My routine is whatever I choose it to be. I can even change my scenery whenever it tickles my fancy. Your house doesn't move and you are imbedded in the town or city you live in. I can island hop the Gulf Coast. I can motor to the Keys. I can take a trip to the Dry Tortugas or the Bahamas, with my house.

I am truly living a dream life. Most of my life I thought it was impossible. Now I am living proof that it is indeed possible. I wouldn't trade places with any living person on this planet. To be fair, there are many things you can do that I cannot. I can't buy a new big screen television, but I don't care. I can't buy a new car, don't need it. I don't have cable or satellite, don't miss it. Dominos can't deliver where I live and there is no McDonalds. I can't go to the movies, but *"every night there's a hell of a lightshow, direct from the Milky Way."*

I own one pair of flip flops and one pair of deck shoes, but mostly I'm barefoot. I no longer have a big comfy recliner to lounge in, but *"I've got a magic chair. It sits on a beach and takes my cares away."***

I don't have a three bedroom, two bath home in a nice neighborhood, but at any time I could have *"a boat in Belize."**** And no matter where I am, I'll always have "Sky, Sand, Water, Moon."*****

I might miss the Super Bowl, but I'll watch dolphins frolicking instead. I'll probably miss the World Series too, but I'll see ospreys flying with fish in their talons. You get to watch your favorite shows. I get to play with manatees.

There are many things that you take for granted that I have given up. I can't zip to the corner store if I run out of milk. In order to go grocery shopping I have to move my entire house many miles until I get someplace

---

*   Jim Morris
**   Del Suggs
***   Kelly McGuire
**** James (Sunny Jim) White

where I can go ashore to re-provision. I take extremely brief showers in order to conserve water, soap up, rinse and done. I can't do that every day either. We don't have an endless water supply. We don't have endless electricity either. Our power comes from batteries that have to be recharged by running a generator or the main engine, so it is rationed as well.

We don't have a washer and dryer. We find a Laundromat or borrow from friends. We wear the same clothes for several days, especially bathing suits. We have on occasion washed clothes in a tub or bucket. Even washing dishes is a creative exercise in water conservation.

Our boat is a mere thirty-six feet long and twelve feet wide. That is smaller than the tiniest mobile home, but we are not confined by it. The whole world is our playground. We go fishing off the front porch and the beach is in our backyard.

We are not impoverished by the things we no longer have. Instead, we are enriched by the beauty that surrounds us. We no longer possess the finest things, but we are happier without them. We no longer pursue the goals that society says will lead to success. We pursue peace, serenity and joy. *"It's kind of hard being*

upwardly mobile, when you're laying in the sun all day."
(Jim Morris)

Two close boyhood friends grow up and go their separate ways. One becomes a humble monk, the other a rich and powerful minister to the King. Years later they meet. As they catch up, the minister (in his fine robes) takes pity on the thin, shabby monk. Seeking to help, he says:

"You know, if you could learn to cater to the King you wouldn't have to live on rice and beans."

To which the monk replies: "If you could learn to live on rice and beans, you wouldn't have to cater to the King."

We no longer cater to the King. If that means eating rice and beans, or hotdogs, or grilled cheese sandwiches . . . so be it. You may feel that we've made great sacrifices in order to follow the path we have chosen, but we don't feel that way at all. By shunning consumerism and embracing minimalism we've created a much more fulfilling life for ourselves. We would never trade the freedom we experience each and every day for the possessions we left behind.

23

THE PLAN

It's a simple life in paradise. This is a simple book. There are plenty of fine books available about the more technical aspects of a life aboard. More experienced cruisers than I have written many books that can help with engines and systems, navigation, provisioning and the like. That's not what I'm trying to do.

I am trying to share my pure enjoyment of a life of freedom and how I made it happen. While most just dream, I actually went out and did it. I've gone through the plan in earlier chapters, but let's put it all together.

Step 1 - Stop Buying Stuff

Step 2 - Pay Off All Your Debt

Step 3 – Save Money

Step 4 – Get Rid Of Your Stuff

Stop buying stuff. I have a saying I use on the boat. If we can't eat it, drink it, or wipe our butts with it, we ain't buying it. That's not completely true of course, there are other necessities we can't eat, like soap and detergent for example. The key word is necessity. It is not necessary to buy more clothes or shoes. It is not necessary to buy more trinkets or gadgets or toys. It is not necessary to eat out, or stop at Starbucks or go to a movie theater. Train yourself to eliminate all unnecessary spending immediately. Take a close look at you personal habits when it comes to spending money. Do you smoke? Maybe you can quit or at least switch to a budget brand. Do you drink? Can you quit, cut back or buy a cheaper brand? Apply this discriminating logic to all of the places you spend money. Can you spend less on cable or satellite? Can you do without it? Can you manage with a cheaper cell phone plan? Once you get serious about reining in unnecessary spending, you'll be surprised at how much extra disposable income you will have.

Use that extra cash to pay off your debt. Again, this is the hard part but it's the most important. You will never have true freedom until you are debt free. Everyone seems to believe we are to carry mortgages, car loans, and credit card debt on our backs until we die. Debt enslaves us. Debt forces you to that miserable job every day. Debt is the enemy. If you want to live the dream, you must defeat debt.

How do you eat an elephant? One bite at a time. Pick one loan or credit card and work it down to zero. Sell things. Apply the money to debt. Quit buying stuff and use any and all extra money to pay off debt. Each time you pay something off, you'll have that much more to apply to the next target. This makes it easier as you go. Car loans, credit cards and personal loans can be made to disappear with diligence.

Home mortgages are a different story. If you owe more than it's worth, that's a real obstacle. Let's say you are paying one thousand dollar a month on a car and credit cards. Once you pay those off, you could apply an extra thousand towards your mortgage. Once you bring the balance in line with it's worth, you can sell without taking a loss.

If you have some equity in your house, put it up for sale now. Rent a smaller, less expensive home until you are ready to run off to your version of paradise.

I'm not particularly qualified to offer advice on real estate matters, but there are other options you may wish to explore, such as short sales or renting out your house. However you decide to do it, the mortgage burden has to be eliminated.

Save money. Congratulations! You stopped buying stuff and paid off your debts. Now you get to watch your savings grow. This was a very rewarding experience for me.

If your employer offers a 401K, you should take full advantage. If your employer has a company match, you need to contribute the maximum percentage of your pay that they will match. This is free money. Build your 401K balance as a nest egg for use later in life. You can also draw from it in case of emergencies, but there is a tax penalty for early withdrawal.

Once I paid off my debt, I put all that extra money into a savings account. You may wish to stuff it in a mattress or bury it in the back yard. Interest on savings is so paltry; there is no income to be made from it. You want to build a big stash of cold hard cash though, so you'll need to put it somewhere safe.

How much cash do you need? That depends on many different factors. What is a reasonable goal based on your income? How close are you to cashing in that 401K without penalty? How close are you to collecting

Social Security? Are you comfortable taking the lesser amount at age sixty-two? What level of comfort do you expect to live in?

For us, choosing to live with only the basic necessities was the only way. We are poor by anyone's standards, but our needs are few. How cheaply could you live with no bills to pay? How cheaply could you live if you only bought things to eat, drink, or wipe your butt with?

We live very inexpensively here in our sunny setting. Our only indulgences are booze for sunset viewing and books. Kim and I are both avid readers, but we are frugal with our book purchases. We take advantage of book swaps that are common among marinas. We trade with friends. We go to used book stores and search Amazon for cheap Kindle titles.

There are lots of ways to control your spending while you are saving up cash. Not spending is a way of saving. Do you subscribe to magazines or newspapers? Cancel those. Ladies you can stop getting those manicures and pedicures. You can also cut back on the trips to the hairstylist or find a cheaper one. Anything that can be classified as a want instead of a need can be eliminated.

Do you still have a home phone and a cell phone? Get rid of the landline if your cell works at home. When is the last time you shopped for car or home insurance? Maybe you can find it for less. Concentrate on buying sale items at the grocery store or select generic brands. Pack a lunch every day. Turn down the heat a few degrees. Turn up the air conditioning in the summer or rely on it less.

Many of us have simply become spoiled. We buy what we want, when we want. We use credit cards for frivolous purposes. We drastically over spend on Christmas. We go to parties hosted by friends to purchase jewelry, handbags and sex toys. We go to a bar and spend four dollars for a beer instead of buying a six pack and taking it home.

If you want to change your life, it's pretty simple. Quit wasting your money. Save money instead. Make it your purpose in life to save money. Save, save, and then save some more. If you never summon the courage to make the break from society like I did, you'll still be much better off. Maybe you have no desire to live on a boat. That's fine. Buy that little cabin in the woods free and clear. Pay cash for a beachfront condo.

Whatever life you desire, it can be achieved if you change the way you think about money. Stop buying stuff, pay off your debt, and save money.

THE PLAN

Once you've changed your ways, gotten out of debt and saved a pile of money, you'll have some decisions to make. How much or little can you live on? Let's say you've decided fifteen thousand per year will do it. You are four years away from cashing your 401K without penalty. Therefore you need at least sixty thousand to support yourself until then. The 401K will support you until you are eligible for Social Security. You also need money to buy a boat. Another decision has to be made. How much to spend on the boat? A nice but small sailboat may cost as little as twenty grand. A small older trawler can be had for forty. We bought a medium sized, older trawler for sixty. If you do what we did, you would need a minimum of one hundred and twenty thousand dollars to make your move. If you want somewhat of a greater comfort zone, shoot for one fifty. It's that simple, if you really want it.

So you find yourself in your early fifties. You are debt free and getting close to your saving goal. You are shopping for the perfect boat and thinking to yourself, "Hey this could really happen for me." There is one more thing you need to do. Get rid of your stuff.

All of those belongings you've accumulated over the years have no place on a boat. Artwork and knick knacks have got to go. Are you storing a bunch of holiday decorations? You don't need them. You've got too many article of clothing, especially winter wear.

All of your stuff has to go. Kim and I each kept a greatly reduced wardrobe. We held onto cookware, laptop, camera and Kindle. I kept a few fishing rods and a small amount of fishing tackle. We held onto a photo album of our wedding and important documents. All the rest we got rid of.

Have a giant yard sale with the main priority of making stuff disappear. The money is just a bonus. List higher value items on Craigslist and be ready to deal. Be generous with donations to Goodwill or other charities. Give to family and friends.

I cannot overemphasize how freeing this was for us. Just as we were enslaved by debt, we were enslaved by our possessions. Divesting ourselves of all of that stuff was like taking off chains. We were no longer slaves to anyone or anything. We were free in every sense.

Maybe someday you'll do the same. Maybe one day, you'll put a beer to your mouth, take 95 south, and head off for the Keys.

24

FLORIDA

Maybe you'll find yourself anchored snugly between the islands of Cayo Costa and Punta Blanca. Pelican Bay is arguably the finest anchorage in all of Florida. We love it and call it home. The general area surrounding Charlotte Harbor and Pine Island Sound has somehow maintained its sanity while the rest of Florida has completely lost its mind.

All states have their own native characteristics that make them unique. There is the rugged individualism of Texas with its urban cowboys and oil wells. There is the liberal collectivism of California, with Hollywood and hippies. Idaho has potatoes. Georgia has peaches.

Sure Florida has oranges and Disney, but is also populated with immigrants from every other state, Canada and several third-world countries. No other state can claim to have a populous as diverse as Florida. It is also the favorite destination of criminals fleeing justice, tax cheats evading the IRS, homeless looking for warmth, and anyone looking for a second chance after wrecking their old life up north.

The migration continues year after year. The perfectly law abiding just want to retire to palm trees and golf courses. The neer-do-wells and miscreants want to blend in to the ragged edges of the seedier side of the Sunshine State while running from their previous misdeeds. They should call this the Schizophrenic State, but it wouldn't look good on the license plates.

Key West used to be the end of the road for runners of questionable character. Somewhere along the line it got crowded and too expensive. The colorful characters started to settle up the chain of Keys, filling in Marathon, then Islamorada and Key Largo. Eventually all of the Keys were saturated with bohemian artists, frustrated writers, street performers and beggars. The North kept spitting out societal misfits like a Pez dispenser so mainland Florida started welcoming them. Then Fidel Castro boosted Miami's population with the gift of tens of thousands of Cuban refugees.

Cocaine took over from marijuana, which had taken over from citrus, and the craziness kicked into high gear. Previously, a good old boy shrimper or fisherman might make a big score running dope, then settle back into legitimate business. It was all pretty low key and no one got shot. Now, you've got Columbian drug lords running the streets with automatic weapons ventilating bodies left and right.

America may be a melting pot, but Florida is a scalding cauldron of demographic diversity. Out of this steaming stew of diverse humanity comes a special kind of crazy news story almost daily. The Floron of the Day will make headlines with the sheer stupidity of their actions. Add alligators, the Everglades, giant pythons, miniature deer, manatees, dolphins, and Disney, and you've mixed up a surreal hodgepodge of looniness unmatched elsewhere in American.

Somehow, the area of southwest Florida where we roam has managed to avoid all that. Crime is low and crazy is minimal. The barrier islands of Sanibel, Captiva and Gasparilla are wealthy and exclusive. They are also notable for their stunning lack of ethnic diversity. Cayo Costa is uninhabited, unless you count park rangers. Useppa Island is so exclusive you can't step foot on it unless you are a member of their club. Don't ask what that costs unless you are a multi-millionaire. All these islands easily rival the Keys in beauty, and their beaches are far superior.

Our adopted hometown of Punta Gorda is simply the finest town I've encountered in my many travels. It is as neat and clean as a picture book. City planners chose not to allow high rise condos or hotels. The long stretch of waterfront is instead mostly parks and open spaces. Spend a few days in Punta Gorda, and you quickly learn that people are happy to be there.

It all feels very safe, and dare I say. . . normal. May it remain forever immune to whatever weirdness virus that has infected the rest of the state.

25

WHAT WOULD YOU GIVE?

We went through the process I've described. We bought our boat and then staked out our own little piece of paradise. We've spent the past thirty months soaking up the sun and marveling at our good fortune. We've had thirty months of glorious freedom and awesome adventure. If it all falls apart tomorrow, I wouldn't change a thing. This time has brought us happiness and contentment few believe possible. We gave up everything we had, but now we have everything we could ever want.

We have a fine boat that treats us as well as we treat her. I love my wife more than the day we married, and she loves me back just the same. There is no end to the variety of wildlife that entertains us daily. We deeply appreciate the raw natural beauty of these unspoiled islands. We practically worship the awe inspiring sunsets we're privileged to witness. We have our own private white-sand, blue water beaches.

What would you give to live like this?

That, dear reader, is the essence of this tale. We gave up everything. Now we have it all. We gave up our home, our furniture, our satellite television, our washer and dryer, and all of our belongings. We left behind forty plus years of familiarity and friendships. Everything we had ever known faded in our review mirror, but we never looked back.

We have been rewarded a hundred times over, in ways we never imagined. We thought our new life was going to be fantastic, but it turned out even better than we envisioned. The strong new friendships we've made in this life are a gift we didn't foresee. At the same time, we've learned to relish the solitude when we are alone together. We can sit on the beach for hours in silence, just enjoying the calm. We can sit and read without a word passing between us, then smile at each other like we are sharing some special secret.

We gradually released the tension and stress that had been our constant companions for so many years. We became experts in the art of relaxation. We lost the need to keep busy all the time. We mastered the skill of doing nothing. We each have our personal serenity and lightness of being that we didn't know existed.

What would you give to live like this?

After learning my story, some people say things like, "I wish I could live like you," or "someday I want to do that." Let me tell you something. Wishing for someday isn't going to make it happen. I suspect some of those folks don't really believe it's possible. The rest simply can't see themselves giving up the life they have.

That's why I wrote this book. I wanted some day-dreamer out there to see that it is possible. I wanted someone too attached to their possessions to rethink what they were working for. I wanted some poor sap shoveling snow in the frozen north to just quit and move someplace warm. I wanted to inspire a well-off couple to change their retirement plans and sail off to the Caribbean. I wanted some debt ridden, overworked, underpaid worker drone to realize he didn't have to do this until he died. I also wanted to show people that some have chosen a different path, one that leads to freedom. I fully realize that not everyone has the desire to follow that path. I'm under no delusion that every-one who reads this will show up in their boat asking for my autograph. Someone might though. That would make it very worthwhile.

Maybe there will be one guy who reads this and decides he really needs to get out of debt. Maybe one woman will read this and figure out it's time to start saving for retirement. At the very least let me stand as a symbol for those who've chosen a different path. If you never get away, can't make the break, know that I am out here living free.

If you do buy that boat, look me up. I'll be sitting on the back of Leap of Faith, with a cold beer in my hand and another on ice for you.

ACKNOWLEDGEMENTS

Jim Morris: First and foremost I must publicly thank Jim, for writing and singing the songs that inspired me.

Bob Zola: Former boss, thanks for all the opportunities to make money, which I promptly spent on boats.

Geri McGowan: Former coworker, who is in the process of quitting her job and buying a boat, thanks for sharing my dream on company time.

All the fine people of Galena, Maryland: I have many fond memories of all the things we did together over the years. Thanks for being my friends.

All the fine people of southwest Florida: The Charlotte Harbor Parrotheads, The gang at the Navagator, the residents of Fisherman's Village Marina; thanks for accepting us into your community and for being so nice to newcomers. We truly appreciate your friendship.

The Lovely Miss Kim: As mentioned earlier, I wouldn't be here without you. Thank you for sharing our dream. I love you.

All lyrics and song excerpts by Jim Morris are reprinted with the permission of Jim Morris.

Fish Head Music

www.Jim-Morris.com

A portion of *Magic Chair* reprinted with the permission of Del Suggs.

Hurricane Hole Music, ASCAP

www.SaltwaterMusic.com

Excerpt from *Key Weird* reprinted with the permission of Robert Tacoma.

Mango Press

ACKNOWLEDGEMENTS

Song title *Boat in Belize* referenced with the permission of Kelly Mcguire.

www.redfishisland.com

Song title *Sky, Sand, Water, Moon* referenced with the permission of James (Sunny Jim) White.

www.sunnyjim.com

Excerpt from *Honorable Mention* reprinted with the permission of Robert Macomber.

www.robertmacomber.com

Pineapple Press, Inc.

Lyrics from *This Is The USA?* reprinted with the permission of Scott Kirby.

www.scottkirby.com